IT'S
TO GREATNESS!

GRAFTED IN

Author of *The Healing Power of The Roots*

DOMINIQUAE
BIERMAN, PhD

Published by *Zion's Gospel Press*
52 Tuscan Way, Ste 202-412
St. Augustine, FL, 32092
shalom@zionsgospel.com
Paperback ISBN: 978-1-953502-21-6
E-Book ISBN: 978-1-953502-22-3

On occasion words such as Jesus, Christ, LORD and God have been changed by the author, back to their original Hebrew renderings, Yeshua, Messiah, Yahveh, and ELOHIM. Bold or italicized emphasis or underlining within quotations is the author's own.

Printed in the United States of America
First Printing October 2004, Second Printing May 2011, Third Printing June 2021

Dedication & Thanksgiving

I would like to dedicate this book to all the future generations of God's children, to both Jews and Gentiles. May they be great as they walk grafted into the olive tree and sanctify the name of Yahveh in their lives, bringing forth many nations to His knowledge.

I am very grateful for my dearly beloved husband and his continual support and encouragement as I go deeper and higher in Yah's calling. He is truly an eagle warrior!

And to my beloved disciples and Kad-Esh MAP Team in Israel and the nations. Your faithfulness, love and encouragement and your hunger for *truth* are a tremendous comfort and inspiration to me. May the blessing of Ruth in Ruth 2:12 be yours forever!

To the wonderful people of our Israel Shofar Convocation September 2004 for your financial support that made it possible for me to print the book quickly. And for the many hours that Kimberly and Ron Furst invested in correcting the manuscript! You all are real troopers!

Last but not least I want to thank my beloved children Adí and Yuval, my gorgeous Israeli 'sabras' as they keep me on my toes to stay true and shun hypocrisy! Though they came back to their mom already in their teens, they have had the commendable maturity to release me to retreat very often, to travel constantly and to write with no interruptions. You are truly the brilliant future of Israel!

As always, all the glory and the honor go to my beloved friend and heavenly Bridegroom, to Yeshua our Jewish Messiah!

Foreword

Walking on the promise land in a wonderful summer sunshine as a Gentile who believe in Jesus Christ the Jewish Messiah, how privileged I counted myself; the sense of belonging and feeling of being a part of the people was awesome. A thought came to my mind, and it was the promise God made to Abraham; "in your Seed shall all the nations of the earth be blessed." Through Jesus Christ who is that seed of Abraham, people from all the nations of the world have become partakers of this promise by faith in Him—Jesus Christ. When I saw the Jew of the nation of Israel and the Ethiopian Jew walking together and living together, I got a picture of what God meant for the church and Israel.

By faith in Jesus we who were of the wild olive tree have found a place in the commonwealth of Israel, the cultivated olive tree. Now we are not wild anymore but part of the cultivated. We have lost our old wild leaves and old roots in the wilderness; we are planted in a new place, taken from what was there already into what is specially made. We have become a new plant from our origin but same with the cultivated plant. In time of pruning we are pruned together, in feeding we are fed from the same root and source. We bear the same quality of fruit, because now the difference between the wild and the cultivated olive trees exist no more, we are one.

There is a task still needed to be accomplished, to bring the fulfillment of the promise to a full maturation.

The Jew who has to accept that the complete fulfillment of the promise is the inclusion of the Gentile church that has been engrafted into them through Christ Jesus whose original and true Hebrew name is Yeshua the Messiah, in that blessing of Abraham. And the Gentile church which has to understand and accept that through Christ the Jewish Messiah we have found and been given a place in the common wealth of Israel, and that to be given a place does not mean to replace. This replacement theology therefore must be discarded for the unity of the Jew and Gentile to move forward through Christ Jesus who is Yeshua. Archbishop Dominiquae Bierman a Jew of the Jews from the stalk of Abraham loves the church of our Lord Jesus Christ (she herself being a believer in Yeshua our Messiah). She has the calling to see the Jew and Gentile believers come together as one people. The misconception of the church concerning the Jews; which led to the atrocities meted to them and the tainting that the Jews have in their minds concerning the church as a result of the pain suffered under the influence of the church is now healed. This book is an eye opening to both the Gentile church and the Jews. I am so glad that God has raised such a woman as Bishop Dominiquae Bierman to bring these truths to print. These truths gave me insight and answers to my questions and have propelled me into seeking to know more about the Jews of whom I have become a part through Jesus Christ who is Yeshua the Jewish Messiah.

I believe that her significant time and efforts, her passion for her people the Jews and for the church of our Lord Jesus Christ, Yeshua, are worth every commendation.

Archbishop J. P. Hackman
President of TAPAC

Do not think that I came to abolish the Law and the Prophets; I did not come to abolish but to interpret it to the full. Whoever then annuls the least of these Commandments, and teaches others to do the same, shall be called least in the Kingdom of heaven; but whoever keeps and teaches them shall be called great in the Kingdom of heaven.

— Matthew 5:17-19

RESTORED TERMINOLOGY

I want to introduce a few terms that I will use throughout the entire book with no further explanation:

Yahveh

Yahveh is the name of the Lord as revealed to Moses and used throughout the prophetic writings. It means "the I AM and the Ever Present God."

This name is often used in conjunction with the name *ELOHIM*, which is the name of the Creator God.

Elohim

The name of the Lord when He is revealing Himself as the Creator. Yahveh ELOHIM, "The I AM who is The Creator"

In the beginning ELOHIM created the heavens and the earth.

— Genesis 1:1

Yah

Translated as God. Yah as in HalleluYah. So, many times I will use the word Yah instead of the word God.

Extol Him that rideth upon the heavens by His name Yah.

— Psalm 68:4

The Torah

Torah is the Hebrew word for "instruction in righteousness," commonly called Law. In this book Torah only refers to the Law of Yahveh in the five books of Moses and throughout the Bible.

In this book, Torah does not refer to any rabbinical Laws or man-made traditions. In a place where I mention a rabbinical tradition, I will refer to it as such.

Because Abraham obeyed my voice, and kept my charge, my Commandments, my statutes and my Laws (Torah).

— Genesis 26:5

Please note that even prior to the giving of the Torah at Mount Sinai, Abraham already walked and obeyed it, because the Torah of the Living Yah is eternal.

Important: The Torah includes three types of Laws:

- Commandments
- Statutes or Judgments
- Laws or Precepts

The Commandments, i.e., the Ten Commandments, are forever.

The statutes are also forever, and they are connected with Holiness and Worship. Following the statutes that are connected with Temple worship requires more knowledge of their background and a Holy Spirit interpretation. This is necessary in order to learn and know how to follow them today through the Spirit who gives life, since we are now the Temple of the Holy Spirit.

The precepts are eternal principles that are relevant and directed to the issues of the time in which they were given, although the actual instructions were temporary. So today we keep the principles and apply it to our times. As we walk with the Holy Spirit of Yah, He continues to give us precepts daily.

The ticket to success and prosperity in life:

This Book of the Law (Torah) shall not depart from your mouth, but you shall meditate on it day and night, that you may observe to do according to all that is written in it. For then you will make your way prosperous, and then you will have good success.

— Joshua 1:8

Abraham, the Father of Faith, understood and walked in the light that he had. In these End times, Yah is restoring to the church what will make us blessed, successful, and prosperous: The Torah as revealed to us by the Holy Spirit. As we meditate on Yah's holy Commandments, Judgments and Precepts, the Word will become flesh in us and will produce the fruit of obedience. Obedience will bring the fullness of the blessing.

Yeshua

Yeshua, commonly called Jesus Christ, is the real Hebrew name for the Jewish Messiah. Yeshua means Yah is our Salvation and it implies Salvation, Deliverance, and

Redemption. Throughout this book, I will only use Yeshua, His true Hebrew name.

Yeshua is the Living Torah, or the Torah made flesh. As you follow Him and His Ruach HaKodesh, His Holy Spirit, He will lead you into all Truth.

And you shall know the truth, and the truth shall make you free.

— John 8:32

CONTENTS

INTRODUCTION

I t has been over 1600 years since the church worldwide lost the original Apostolic Jewish biblical foundations of the gospel of the Kingdom. Since the year 325 at the time of the signing of the Council of Nicaea. The church has been partially and at times totally disconnected from the original gospel of the Kingdom as preached by the Jewish Apostles, the original 12 Church Fathers. This disconnection or divorce has cost the lives of millions of Jews that have been exterminated in the name of Christ due to the replacement theology, that followed the Council of Nicaea. It has also cost the lives of all the nations of the earth, that have suffered from a serious curse due to the church's disconnection from its Jewish Roots and the following hatred towards the Jewish people and even towards the Holy Hebrew Scriptures as well! The promise in Genesis 12:3 as given to Abraham and to his descendants (Israel, the Jews) is pending over the nations. The Tick Tack of the End time heavenly clock is marking the last eternal seconds before the closing of this age and the outpouring of the wrath of God, prior to His Second coming. (Please see Appendix 1 at the end of the book)

"I will bless those that bless you. I will curse those who curse you"

The Ecclesia[1] must be restored to the greatness that the Early Church in Jerusalem had and even more!

Before the closing of this age the Father Almighty desires to pour His glory on all nations, so that many can be saved.

In order for that to happen there is a need to *repent* and *reject* the Council of Nicaea and all traces of *replacement theology*. There is an urgent need to be restored to the Original Apostolic Jewish foundations as the early church was, and break all the curses that replacement theology has brought to the church and to the nations.

The entire church needs to humble herself and pass through a 'baptism of repentance and of cleansing.' Then and only then will she move on into the greatness and the glory and will be effective in the restoration of Israel and in the salvation of the nations.

When the spirit of the Council of Nicaea leaves the church, many Jews will accept Yeshua and many nations will come into the Kingdom. As we go all over the world with this message, followed by End time signs, wonders and miracles, we see Gentiles and Christians saved, transformed and restored and many Jews enter into the Kingdom with great ease. Following the repentance and the outpouring of

---

1   The Ecclesia is the Greek word for congregation, often translated as Church.

His glory, there has to be a changed lifestyle into obedient Kingdom living, and greatness.

This book has been written in order to help you, the repentant, humble and hungry reader to be restored to the early church lifestyle. As you do, you will walk in Yah's greatness and glory all the days of your life.

For those that humble their hearts to this metamorphosis, cleansing and restoration, there will be a glorious empowering for the End time work that is at hand. And they will be followed with amazing signs, wonders and miracles! I suggest that you read my books "The Healing Power of The Roots" and "Sheep Nations" in order to help you with the metamorphosis and reformation and receive the full understanding of its importance.

Your friend and His Archbishop;
Dr. Dominiquae Bierman, Israel

"For the Law shall go forth from Zion and the Word of Yahveh from Jerusalem"

— Isaiah 2:3

CHAPTER ONE:

Grafted In

"But if some of the branches were broken off and you, being a wild olive, were grafted in among them and became partaker with them of the rich root of the olive tree, do not be arrogant against the branches; but if you are remembered that it is not you who supports the root, but the root supports you."

— Romans 11:17-18

We were in a mission's conference in a Latin American country and the host was emphasizing the need for recovering the lost cultures of the nations. He desired to incorporate their music and dance expressions into the body of Messiah.

What a beautiful and noble idea, I said to myself as I pondered about this burning vision in His heart. How powerful and rich it is to incorporate the Maori and Latino beat with the European and the African music style.

Being a psalmist and very musical myself I whole heartedly agreed with the need of joining and adding all

1

sanctified expressions of ethnic worship. However, the key word is sanctified expressions as not all ethnic worship is holy.

Later on, I witnessed firsthand in the same conference many unsanctified expressions on stage that reminded me of lustful dancing in some ethnic disco clubs, when the men and the women twirl their body in front of each other in voluptuous movements and with seductive looks. As Christian ladies dressed with short miniskirts and very tiny and uncovered blouses, often displaying their bellies or part of their breasts rose to dance in front of excited Christian men, supposedly in an attempt to recover the worship expressions of the nations, the Holy Spirit said to me:

"...And they rose to play."[1]

My spirit was grieved to the core as I watched the leadership of the said conference joining in and encouraging such perversion on stage! Later on, when we tried to go back to the meeting hall as a sign of grace towards the ignorance of the organizers, the Holy God of Israel did not permit us. Right outside of the meeting hall the Holy Spirit, who is the Spirit of Holiness, fell on us and on our team and everyone that joined us or even came close. The Most High was making His holy altar outside of the main meeting hall of the said conference. People around us began weeping and breaking; they fell on the floor, some drunk with the Holy

---

1 Incident of the Golde Calf found in Exodus 32:6

Spirit. Some even began to laugh and receive healing. One young man, a pastor, began to cry out loud:

Please God, give me a love for Israel that I do not have. I want to love Israel!

Later on, he reported to us that a new love for Israel had been birthed in His heart. One of the women present, the leader of a missions and intercession team, took the shoes off her feet and I followed her. This was holy ground.

The Holy Scriptures tell us that the Gentiles were wild olive branches. In other words, their cultural expressions needed to become grafted into the cultivated olive, Israel, and needed to go through a metamorphosis and become like the natural tree, leaving all 'wildness' behind. There is a great difference between exuberant holy worship and the wild expressions of the nations.

I have been a witness to some beautiful worship expressions from some African brethren and especially from the First Nations of North America, also called the American Indians. With every drum beat and every step of their dance the glory of Yah was released. There was nothing voluptuous or seductive in their dancing. Theirs was holy praise! But I also know the leader who comes to Israel very often and loves to drink from the rich root of the olive tree.

I would like to stress here again that I am not rejecting the cultural expressions of the nations. On the contrary, I love them, as long as they are sanctified and Holy Spirit inspired. That is possible only when Gentile believers are *grafted into* the olive tree and allow themselves to become *cultivated* in that *tree* and nourished by its rich root! In other words, there is a need to allow the Torah, Yah's instructions in righteousness, God's laws, as interpreted by the Holy Spirit who is the Spirit of Holiness to be written in all our hearts.

I remember when I had just accepted the Messiah, a brother from England came to my home in Jerusalem. As he looked at the paintings on my walls, he was obviously disturbed and told me that they were demonic. Because I was only a few days old in the Messiah, I still could not discern well enough. I got quite offended; however, I made it a point to pray about it. As I sat in my living room looking at the paintings and praying, the Spirit of Holiness fell upon me and I began to remove and tear apart all those pictures! I had painted them myself under the influence of another spirit, a New Age spirit prior to my salvation. They were abstract but still had the influence of the wrong spirit. I had to throw away all 'my art expression' because they were of *another* spirit. I did the same with my writings. I was writing a book at that time about some dramatic events in my life. A few days after my new birth, I was reading the book, and I knew that I needed to burn it. So, all my art expressions ended in the fire because they were of *another* spirit! It is the same with the cultural expressions of the nations. All things need to be tested:

"But examine everything carefully, hold fast to that which is good. Abstain from every form of evil."

— 1 Thessalonians 5:21, 22

Let us take a look at a very sobering instruction given to the people of Israel (The cultivated olive tree!) prior to possessing the promised land:

"Be careful to listen to all these words which I command you, so that it may be well with you and your Sons after you forever, for you will be doing what is right in the sight of Yahveh your Elohim. When Yahveh your Elohim cuts off before you the nations which you are going in to dispossess them and dwell in their land, beware that you are not ensnared to follow them, after they are destroyed before you, and that you do not inquire after their Gods, saying "How do these nations serve their Gods, that I may also do likewise? You shall not behave thus towards Yahveh your Elohim, for every abominable act which Yahveh hates they have done for their Gods; for they even burn their Sons and their daughters in the fire to their Gods. Whatever I command you (in how to worship Me), you shall be careful to do; you shall not add nor take away from it."

— Deuteronomy 12:28-32

Yahveh is warning Israel not to try to use the 'style' of worship of the nations in order to worship Him. In other words, there is a *unique heavenly style* of worship that comes directly from Him. There is no need to 'borrow from the devil' in order to worship God. Yah is not an imitator; He is a Creator and originator! That is why, He said to Abram in Genesis 12:1,

"Now Yahveh said to Abram: "Go forth from your country and from your relatives and from your father's house to the land that I will show you."

— Genesis 12:1

What He was telling Abram was to *let go* of his own culture and his own inheritance, his own style of worship and follow the Creator, the great *I AM* to a land and to a lifestyle that He would show him. The Word tells us that every Gentile who comes to the knowledge of Messiah is a child of Abraham by faith. Many people like to claim that, but they hardly understand what that means! It means that every Gentile needs to do what Abraham did, and by faith leave all their old lifestyle behind and follow the God of Abraham to a land that they do not know. That land is the olive tree, the same biblical, Hebrew culture as given to Israel. The manual and the road map of that land is the Hebrew Holy Scriptures, including the Torah or Law, the Prophets and the Writings. The guide that takes us to that land and instructs us there according to the road map is the Holy Spirit. Abraham had to leave everything and learn *another* way and so does every believer from the nations who comes to faith in the Jewish Messiah, Yeshua.

It is grafted into the olive tree that all that is godly within the nations will come to fruition and what a beautiful and tasty fruit that will be!

An Important Disclaimer

Please notice that I did not say that Gentiles needed to be grafted into the Jewish Religion but rather to the Hebrew or Jewish biblical culture as in the Holy Scriptures. There are many people who have taken this message wrongly and they are trying to copy Jewish cultural expressions that are not necessarily biblical or anointed and they are trying to be more orthodox than the orthodox Jews. Though there may be much beauty in that, I am not talking about copying some more cultural expressions. I am rather challenging you, the reader to return to the original Hebrew Holy Scriptures and to allow the Holy Spirit to write His laws and instructions in your heart. Being grafted into the olive tree does not mean to be grafted into another religious system but rather into a nation called Israel and into the biblical lifestyle that is fashioned by the manual that shaped that nation from the beginning—the Bible! Please bear with me as in a later chapter I will explain how to relate to the Hebrew Holy Scriptures in a correct manner when you are a true New Testament believer. This marvelous book of instruction has been called "Old Testament" incorrectly since the council of Nicaea and it has been taken very lightly and dishonored. By the end of this book you will understand its importance and you will know how to read it and profit from all of it!

Let us worship the Father in Spirit and truth, with African beat and the Latino passion, the Maori intensity and the Native American depth. However, let us remember that it is not only in Spirit but also in truth. The truth as found in the Holy Hebrew Scriptures and as revealed to us by the Spirit of truth!

"Stand in the way and look for the ancient paths, where the good way is, and you will find rest for your souls."

An Important Fact

Most of the Jewish people today are very far from their own Hebrew-biblical culture, and they themselves need to be restored to their own olive tree and its roots. But that does not negate the calling of the Ecclesia to be grafted in! And when she is, she will fulfill her calling to make the Jews jealous to have their Messiah back. This End time grafted in church will be able to be an agent of healing to the Jewish people for all the terrible wounds and sufferings inflicted upon her in the name of Christ (Romans 11:14). However, the good news is that in this End time of transformation, the Father is raising up some redeemed Jews, Apostolic and Prophetic Jews that will help the church to become grafted in again as she was two thousand years ago. Then all the nations together with the Jewish people will worship the Father in Spirit and truth.

"Elohim be gracious unto us and bless us and cause His face to shine upon us-Selah. That Your way may be known on the earth, Your salvation among all nations."

— Psalms 67: 1, 2

What Is the Importance of the Grafting?

In the true gospel the nations, the Gentiles are grafted into the Jewish tree and not vice versa. The word *grafting* is very revealing as it explains the magnitude of the joining between Jew and Gentile in the same tree, in the same Hebrew biblical culture where the Holy ethnic expressions of all nations can be fully appreciated and sanctified. Yeshua spoke of this grafting in the book of John as He said:

"I do not ask on behalf of these alone, but for those also who believe in Me through their word. That they may all be one; even as You Father are in Me and Me in You, that they also may be in Us, so that the world may believe that You sent Me." John 17:20-21

When He spoke these words, there were only Jewish disciples then; and He prophesied that 'others', namely the Gentiles would believe through their word! He prayed that these 'others' (the Gentiles) would become *one* with the Jewish believers. That this *oneness* is the same as the unity between Yeshua and His Father, and that this *oneness* between Jew and Gentile believer in the same Messiah would cause the world to believe in Him. In other words, without this unity the world would not believe in Messiah! So, the strategy for the salvation of the world was, is and will be the unity that happens when Gentiles join with the Jews in the same Kingdom, in the same olive tree! Please note that I did not say that the unity depended on the Jews joining the

Gentiles in a Christian made tree but rather that the Gentiles need to join the believing Jews in the olive tree, Israel's tree!

This is the key issue that will turn the church, that will cause Israel to be jealous to have Messiah back and that will cause the salvation of the nations!

When Emperor Constantine from Eastern Rome wrote the Council of Nicaea in year 325, which was endorsed by the Gentile church fathers of the time, he said:

Let us separate from the detestable company of the Jews because the Savior has shown us another way. Our worship following a more convenient course..."

He was saying; Let us Gentiles *not* be grafted into this Jewish olive tree, with its Hebrew roots and biblical culture! *Rather* let us follow what we *like* and is more *familiar* and *convenient* to us. Let us follow our Gentile culture! In other words, *let us stay wild olive branches and reject the in-grafting!* That is exactly what has happened to the church since then. By rejecting the grafting into the cultivated olive tree, the church has remained in the wild olive of the culture of the nations, in the Babylonian-Greco-Roman religious system, with its pagan traditions, pagan feasts and heathen terminology and thus has not born the fruit that Yahveh intended for her to bear if she would have been grafted into His olive tree—Israel.

Think about it: why would an African or an American be celebrating the Babylonian feast of Ishtar called Easter or the celebration of the Babylonian God Tamuz, now called

Christmas², when trees are decorated? Why are they not celebrating the biblical feasts given to Israel and through Israel to all the nations? Why would all the believers from all the nations have exactly the same culture as it pertains to celebrating "Christian Holidays?" Shouldn't they have the Hebrew culture in common, the one that comes from the olive tree and those feasts that Yahveh calls *my holy feasts*? "...But this is the result of the council of Nicea and of replacement theology. All the nations through the church in the nations are now polluted with Babylonian pagan worship and it is called "Christian."³All the nations saved, and unsaved people know and celebrate Christmas, Easter and even Halloween. Can you imagine if all the nations through a grafted in church would learn about Yah's holy feasts that demonstrate Him and testify of Him? All nations would celebrate Passover and Pentecost (Shavuot) and Tabernacles (Sukkot). All nations would keep and honor the Shabbat and make it holy and what a blessing that would be to the nations! (Leviticus 23)

"Many nations will come and say, come and let us go up to the mountain of the Lord and to the house of the God of Jacob, that He may teach us

---

2   For more information about the pagan origins of Christmas, Easter and Halloween please read my books *The Healing Power of the Roots* and *Sheep Nations* and see the appendix at the end of the book.

about His ways and that we may walk in His paths. For from Zion will go forth the Law and the Word of the Lord from Jerusalem."

— Micah 4:2

The Difference Between the Olives!

First of all let us read this Scripture again:

"But if some of the branches were broken off and you, being a wild olive, were grafted in among them and became partaker with them of the rich root of the olive tree, do not be arrogant against the branches; but if you are remembered that it is not you who supports the root, but the root supports you."

— Romans 11:17, 18

In this verse we read that *some* of the Jewish branches, the original branches were broken off. Some, not all! Then we read that Yahveh brought *other* branches to be grafted in among them, not *instead* of them. In many translations it says: Instead of them, in other words replacing them, replacing the Jews. This translation from the NAS is faithful to the original where it says that Gentiles were brought into the olive tree among and together with the Jews in their olive tree. Gentiles become partaker, which means that they share with the Jews of the *rich root* of the tree. So, Gentiles do not replace the Jews but join the Jews and become one with them!

The difference between a wild olive and a cultivated olive is huge. A wild olive grows on the surface without any roots. Though it multiplies a lot and very fast its leaves are very small and insignificant, and its fruit is non-edible. Its fruit, the wild olive is thin and small. It has no oil and no meat; it is only skin and bone. If you try to eat a wild olive, you would break your teeth and go away disgusted and hungry. The wild olives can be uprooted very easily, and they do not stand strong winds and storms; because their fruit is unusable, they are a bother as they take up space and can be used for nothing, not even for beauty as they look very unkempt.

However, the cultivated olive is very different as it is characterized by a complex root system that goes down quite deep. Its roots become so strong that I have seen some of them breaking through walls and stone. They take longer to grow and to develop good fruit, but they practically live forever. Storms and strong winds cannot uproot them as their roots are so deep and strong. I have seen olive trees in Israel that are so old that some think that they were probably there when Yeshua walked the Land of Israel! The leaves of these trees are shiny and very beautiful. They look like they are covered with silver and the fruit is heavenly. Their fruit is plump, meaty and full of wonderful olive oil. Cultivated olive trees nourish many people, their leaves have healing properties and so does the oil. You would rarely find a true Middle Eastern salad without olives in it! The cultivated olive is likened unto the Tree of Life that is mentioned in Revelation 22:1, 2:

"Then He showed me a river of the water of life, clear as crystal coming from the throne of God and from the lamb. In the middle of its street, on either side of the river was the tree of life, bearing twelve kinds of fruit, yielding its fruit every month; and the leaves of the tree were for the healing of the nations."

— Revelation 22:1, 2

What an awesome description of the beauty and goodness of this tree.

The Grafting Process

Our personal assistant, Daniel, is a landscaper and a gardener and he knows a lot about grafting. This is what a professional Swiss gardener confirmed to me:

In order to graft a wild branch into a cultivated tree, the original tree needs to be wounded and the wild branch is introduced into that open place. Then as it stays there, the first reaction is that the grafted in branch loses all of its small leaves and non-edible fruit. The grafted branch becomes naked or bare because its former 'fruit' and leaves are not compatible with the cultivated olive. As the graft remains with its new tree, it begins to suck the nourishment from the rich root of this olive tree, and it begins to revive and to become green and healthy. Sometime later new, shiny and beautiful silvery leaves appear and then; the fruit! When the Cultivated Fruit shows up, then the graft 'knows' that it was all worth it. The fruit is plump, meaty and *full* of oil, the beautiful *olive oil* that is used in the Holy Scriptures as anointing oil and healing oil. No more skin and bone, no more broken teeth and unusable fruit, this time the fruit is glorious! Now, when the grafting is completely finished and successful, there is absolutely *no difference* between the grafted-in branch and the original branches. The ex-wild branch has nothing left of its wildness and its fruit is identical to the one from the original tree. *Grafting* is a very delicate and important process. This is what the Apostle Yaakov (James) meant in Acts 15 at the Jerusalem Council when he gave four laws to the gentiles coming into the olive tree:

"Therefore, it is my judgment that we do not trouble those who are turning to God from among the gentiles. But that we write to them that they abstain from things contaminated by idols and from fornication and from what is strangled and from blood. For Moses from ancient generations has in every city those who preach him, since he is read in the synagogues every Sabbath."

— Acts 15:19-21

The grafted in branch becomes one with the cultivated tree!

Grafting is a very delicate and important process. This is what the Apostle Yaakov (James) meant in Acts 15 at the Jerusalem council when he gave four laws to the Gentiles coming into the olive tree:

"Therefore, it is my judgment that we do not trouble those who are turning to God from among the gentiles. But that we write to them that

they abstain from things contaminated by idols and from fornication and from what is strangled and from blood. For Moses from ancient generations has in every city those who preach him, since he is read in the synagogues every Sabbath."

— Acts 15:19-21

Let me paraphrase this Scripture to you in the context of the *grafting*:

"Therefore, it is my judgment that we do not make it hard on those that are turning to God from among the gentiles, since they need to go through the grafting process and lose all their pagan lifestyle in order to become one with us in the same olive tree. Let us instruct them to leave the most serious heathen and wild behavior such as the worship of other Gods, sex outside of Holy matrimony, eating in an unclean way, that is profane such as strangled animals and consuming blood that is a sacrilege. And since they will go through the process of grafting into us (losing all their unusable leaves and non-edible fruit, pagan traditions and unruly behavior), they will come to the synagogues every Shabbat where they will learn the rest of the Torah (Five Books of Moses) and as they partake of the rich root of the olive tree with us they will begin to receive life and Godliness. The Holy Spirit will write the Torah-laws in their heart and they will become one of us and one with us!"

That they may all be one; even as You Father are in Me and Me in You, that they also may be in Us, so that the world may believe that You sent Me."

— John 17:20-21

CHAPTER TWO:

The Anti-Messiah Exposed

"Thus, He said: 'the fourth beast will be a fourth Kingdom on the earth, which will be different from all the other Kingdoms and will devour the whole earth and tread it down and crush it. As for the ten horns, out of this Kingdom ten kings will arise; and another will arise after them, and he will be different than the previous ones and will subdue three kings. He will speak out against the Most High and will wear down the saints of the Highest One, and he will make alterations in times and in law; and they will be given into his hand for a time, times and half a time."

— Daniel 7:23-25

In the Book of Daniel, we can find invaluable information about the end of times and about the different Kingdoms and systems that affect the world. We can see here that Daniel talks here about a fourth beast that is different than the other ones. This fourth beast is a fourth Kingdom that affects the whole earth. This fourth beast is the Kingdom of

Rome. The other three Kingdoms before it, were: Babylon, Persia and Greece. Rome was indeed different and though the Roman Empire was defeated yet its effects are felt unto this day and especially in and through the church. The Roman Empire has indeed devoured the whole earth through Emperor Constantine who was a type of Antichrist as he altered the laws and the seasons of the Most High when he divorced the church of his time from the Jews and the biblical Jewish Roots and holy feasts through the Council of Nicea.

When Constantine came into power as the king of Eastern Rome, also called Byzantium, he made a truce with the believers in Messiah and promised them peace and safety if they were willing to reject the grafting into the Hebrew olive tree and to become Gentile/Pagan again. He was very clear in his approach to the former wild olives. He said that they will not suffer any more persecution if they were willing to submit to him as the head of the church, or its first Pope. When the Gentile church fathers agreed with him, he proceeded to uproot every trace of Hebrew, Jewish, biblical olive tree roots out of the Gentile portion of the church. The Jewish believers of the time were outnumbered by the Gentile believers and their voice and opinion was drowned in the midst of the noise of compromise. They were given an ultimatum: Either become a compromised, pagan Christian like all of us Gentiles and you get 'grafted into our Roman culture' or you are out! Many Jewish believers were ostracized out of the mainline church at that time and many lost their lives defending the eternal values of the Holy Scriptures. In year 325 the act of 'de-grafting' or uprooting the church from the olive tree was formalized and from that moment, replacement theology begins to rule the body and all traces of Judaism are removed from the church and from the Messiah Himself! Yeshua's name is officially banned and instead of His holy name given to Him by His Father, YHVH, now this apostate church changes its name to a derivative of the highest pagan deity-Zeus. Thus, Yeshua is changed to the Roman form— *Jesus*. Jesus is not a translation of Yeshua which means: Salvation, Healing, Deliverance, but rather another form of saying *Zeus*, so that the people can understand that this Lord is the highest Lord just like Zeus or Jupiter is the highest God in Greek and Roman religion. But no, dear people! Yeshua cannot be compared to any idol or false God, He is higher and the highest and His name is *holy, unchangeable and immutable*! Just like the name of His Father YHVH, the *I AM* is holy, unchangeable and immutable. This Roman Christianity also changed the name of the Father to JEHOVA, however, that is not His name either, but YHVH which in Hebrew is comprised of two words: Yah—the eternal name of God Most High like in *HaleluYah* (Praise to Yah!) and HVEH, which means *present* or *continually being*. YHVH, the *I AM* that *is and was and is to come*.

Replacement Theology is the Spirit of Anti-Messiah

Since the Council of Nicaea and the divorce of the church from the cultivated olive tree, replacement theology has been ruling in the church to one degree or another. Replacement theology is the very spirit of the Antichrist that the Scriptures warn us about. Let us see the essence of the anti-Messiah as described in 1 John 4: 1-3,

"Beloved, do not believe every spirit, but test the spirits to see whether they are from God, because many false prophets have gone out into the world. By this you know the Spirit of God (YHVH!); every spirit that confesses that Yeshua (or Yahshua) the Messiah, the Anointed One has come in the flesh is from God. Every spirit that does not confess Yeshua (that came in the flesh) is not from God; this is the spirit of the Antichrist (anti-Messiah, anti-Anointed), of which you have heard that is coming and now it is already in the world"

— 1 John 4: 1-3

Let me explain this Scripture to you: Apostle John is telling us here a few things:

1. Not to believe every spirit or spiritual doctrine.
2. Test the spirits and the spiritual doctrines to see if they are from God.
3. Many False Prophets have gone out to deceive with false doctrines.
4. There is one way to know that a doctrine is from the Spirit of God.
5. A spirit or spiritual doctrine must confess that Yeshua came as a *man*.
6. A spiritual doctrine that does not relate to the humanity of Yeshua is not from God.

A spiritual doctrine that does not confess that Yeshua came as *a man* is of the Antichrist, which means *it opposes* the Messiah, is an enemy of the Messiah and it rejects *the anointing* and the Holy Spirit.

Since the humanity of Yeshua is so central to be able to discern between holy doctrine and Antichrist doctrine, it is necessary that we know him as a man as well, and not only as God or as YHVH. *Yeshua is YHVH.*

Yeshua is God but His humanity is as important as His divinity in order to maintain the right spirit and a holy doctrine.

Yeshua as a Man

As we open the first book of the gospels, we encounter already in chapter one the genealogy of Yeshua. The writer takes the time to be very thorough to show us His lineage all the way from Abraham and through King David.

"Jacob was the father of Joseph the husband of Miriam, by whom Yeshua was born, who is called the Messiah." Matthew 1:17

The humanity of Yeshua is so important that the whole New Testament portion of the Bible opens up with His human lineage as a Jew.

Later on, we can see the same happening in the last book of the New Testament, in the Book of Revelation that Yeshua being a Jew is *the Key* for His ability to be able to open the Book of Judgment and its seals:

"Then I began to weep greatly because no one was found worthy to open the book or to look into it. And one of the elders said to me: 'Stop

weeping; behold the Lion that is from the tribe of Judah, the Root of David, has overcome so as to open the book and its seven seals."

— Revelation 5:4, 5

The writer of the Book of Revelation makes it a point to describe the only one that has overcome, the only one that has the rights to release judgment on this earth! And this one is described in detail as a Jew, the Lion from the tribe of Judah, the Root of David. Why didn't He say: the Son of God, or the holy child? Why did He have to make a point that this lion is Jewish and of David's lineage?

Because the Son of God came in the flesh as a Jew from the tribe of Judah and from the lineage of David, to sit on the throne of Israel and through Israel rule all humanity! He is the most Jew of all Jews; He is the king of the Jews and anyone that removes His Judaism from Him is functioning under the spirit of anti-Messiah. And that is what Constantine did together with the Gentile church fathers of the fourth century, they removed all traces of Judaism from the Messiah, from His holy name, from the name of His Father, from the church and from all its traditions and celebrations. Constantine and the church fathers instituted replacement theology under the spirit of anti-Messiah and replaced everything Jewish for everything Roman and Babylonian. Until this day the church at large is polluted with the spirit of anti-Messiah in its doctrines as most of it is still utterly disconnected from Israel, from the cultivated olive tree and from the Messiah Yeshua as a Jew.

Many people are praying: Lord, I want to be more like you! Well, He is a Jew! In order to be like Him, we need to get re-grafted into the cultivated olive tree and lose all replacement theology leaves and fruit, all pagan traditions and unholy feasts. Then we will become like Him, the Lion of Judah!

Please listen to what the Word means in 1 John 4:1-3: Any spirit or spiritual doctrine that denies that Yeshua came in the flesh as a Jew and decreases the centrality of Him being a Jew even to this day in heaven, every doctrine like that is of the spirit of the Antichrist or anti-Messiah; anti-Messiah meaning anti-anointed one (Anti-anointing! True Holy Spirit power!). Any doctrine like that needs to be rejected and renounced, repented of and delivered from the spirit of the Antichrist that comes with it, otherwise there will be *no glory* and *no End Time anointing!*

Changing the Name

By far one of the most serious changes introduced by the theologians of replacement theology was the change of His name. In the Book of Acts, we read:

"And there is salvation in no one else; for there is no other name under heaven that has been given among men by which we must be saved."

— Acts 4:12

In other words, His *name* is very important and related to our ability to receive salvation! This is the reason why

His original, Hebrew name, which is His *only true* name, is; Yeshua or Yah (God) is our salvation. *Jesus* is *not* a translation of *Yeshua* but rather another name altogether as Jesus in Greek does not mean "*God is our Salvation.*" Jesus means *God is like Zeus,* the highest God in the Greco-Roman religious system and is also another form of calling Baal, the ancient pagan God whom Elijah the prophet confronted and defeated on Mount Carmel.

JE-is derived from Yah and SUS is derived from *seus* or *Zeus*. In other words, this name was coined in order to let the Romans understand who *Yeshua* is, however, how can the God of Israel be compared with Zeus? We are not saved through a God like Zeus but rather through Yah who is our Salvation! What a difference! Satan has always tried to reduce Yah to his level and exalt himself above Him; that is why he was thrown out of heaven by the Most High. This name was changed on purpose in order to remove any traces of Hebrew or Jewish even from the holy name of Messiah.

"I have heard what the prophets have said who prophesy falsely in My name...Who intend to make My people forget My name by their dreams which they relate to one another, just as their fathers forgot My name because of Baal."

— Jeremiah 23:25-27

The Father has answered the prayers of many that have been praying in *Jesus* name because of their ignorance. However, in these end of times He is requiring from us to repent from all ignorance and to *restore* His rightful name—YHVH-*Yeshua*. In the name of *Jesus Christ* different ethnic groups, and mainly Jewish people have been persecuted, tortured and exterminated; however, no one has been killed in His true name *Yeshua*. Glory be to His holy name that has been kept pure and clean from all defilement! Now He is calling His holy bride to take upon her lips His holy name, thus removing the names of foreign Gods (such as Seus-Zeus) from her holy lips.

"It will come about in that day, declares Yahveh, that you will call me ISHI (my husband) and will no longer call me BAALI (my BAAL-Zeus-Seus). For I will remove the names of the BAALS from her mouth, so that they will be mentioned by their name no more."

— Hosea 2:16, 17

Entire people groups that have never responded to the gospel will now respond because it will be preached in the name of Yeshua rather than *Jesus*. Until this day both Jews and other ethnic groups shiver at the name of *Jesus Christ* as it is connected with horrible massacres and bloodshed and it is *not* the Messiah's name. For a long time, He has answered the prayers of those who are truly His in spite of their ignorance of His true name but now, He is preparing His holy bride and is bringing about the restoration of all things![4]

---

4   Please note that the name of Satan was not changed and remains the same in every language, so what reason is there to change the Holy Name of Yah? The purpose was that His people will forget His name, the most powerful name in the universe!

"And Yahveh will be king over all the earth; in that day Yahveh will be *only One*, and His name will be the *only One*."

— Zechariah 14:9

Let Us Pray

Dear Father in Heaven, thank you for being so merciful to me. I ask Your forgiveness for any spiritual doctrine that I have believed that has voided Yeshua the Messiah from His humanity as a Jew. I most particularly ask you to forgive me for not using Your *true* holy name Yeshua.

I ask Your forgiveness for partaking of any form of replacement theology and for rejecting the grafting into the cultivated olive tree which is Israel. I ask Your forgiveness for staying a wild olive! From now on I reject and renounce all replacement theology and any anti-Messiah doctrine and I receive you *Yeshua* as a Jew into my heart and life.

Please come in and *graft me in completely* into the cultivated olive tree. I willingly lose all wild leaves and fruits, Roman customs and Babylonian traditions so that I can partake of the *rich root* of the olive tree with my Jewish brothers and sisters. I gladly receive Your holy name back YHVH-*Yeshua*!

Let all curses that replacement theology has brought into my life be broken *now*, and let the spirit of anti-Messiah leave me now and never come back! I am Yours forever Yeshua, Jewish Messiah and Your people, the Jews are my people. In Yeshua's Holy Name. Amen.

CHAPTER THREE:

Altering the Seasons and the Laws

"He will speak out against the Most High and will wear down the saints of the Highest One, and he will make alterations in times and in law; and they will be given into his hand for a time, times and half a time."

— Daniel 7:25

n the previous chapter we learnt that Constantine voided the Messiah from His Judaism as he established replacement theology to *replace* the holy gospel of the Kingdom. As he did that he fell into the category of the antichrist or the anti-Messiah spirit. His Antichrist system is also revealed through the fact that he changed or altered the times, or the seasons established by the Creator from the beginning of times.

"Then Elohim said, "Let there be lights in the expanse of the heavens to separate the day from the night, and let them be for signs and for seasons and for days and years;"

— Genesis 1:14

Notice that the Creator already separated the times and the seasons at creation. This I will call creational law. The words that the Hebrew uses for *seasons* are the word *Moadim*, which means *testimonials*. In other words, these are times when the Creator gives testimony of Himself.

These are times when the God of the universe shows up and demonstrates who He is!

No wonder that the devil through the spirit of anti-Messiah would want to alter the times. The altering of the times would cause the people of the Most High to be off course by not waiting for Him and waiting on Him and seeking Him at the times that He appointed to show up.

"Yahveh spoke again unto Moses, saying, "speak to the Sons of Israel and say to them, Yahveh's appointed times which you shall proclaim as Holy convocations-My appointed times are these"

— Leviticus 23:1

Here the Most High is expounding on what He spoke in Genesis 1:14 and in the Hebrew, He uses the exact same word, the word Moadim as in seasons in Genesis 1:14. Here it is *Moadim* for *appointed times*; and to make sure that we understood Him, He said it was *His appointed times,*

His Moadim, His testimonials twice! Then He proceeds to enumerate His Moadim, beginning with the Shabbat and going through all the biblical feasts or the Jewish feasts.

Since we already understand that *Moadim* means *testimonials*, that they are *appointed* by YHVH himself, we can realize that no one has the rights to *disappoint them!* However, since creation there is one that has tried to lift himself up above the Most High and to sit on His throne: that is Satan (Isaiah 14:12-15). And Satan operates through the anti-Messiah spirit and the anti-Messiah religious system established by Constantine and the Gentile church gathers of ancient times. When they altered the times and exchanged the original Moadim for pagan and Roman-Babylonian festivals, it gave Satan the right to seat on the throne of YHVH in the temple of YHVH on *earth*, which is the *church* or the *ecclesia*.

Since Satan was cast out of heaven when he tried to usurp the throne of the Most High (Luke 10:18, Revelation 12:9, Isaiah 14:15), he has always been looking to sit on the throne on earth. He did it through Adam in the garden of Eden and when Yeshua came and took his power and his stolen throne away, he tried to do it again and this time through the seat of power of Yah on earth—the church! He used Constantine and replacement theologians who hated the Jews and everything Jewish. Later on, he used his power in the divorced church to persecute torture and kill Jews wherever the church went. It would be easy to say that this was the catholic church only; however, dearly beloved, it is not so. Satan has been ruling through replacement theology inside of nearly every denomination of Christianity. Since altering the times is of the spirit of the Antichrist, every church or Christian who celebrated altered times such as Sunday, Christmas, Easter and Good Friday are actually engaging the spirit of anti-Messiah.

That is why revivals die! The spirit of anti-Messiah kills them every time that believers are about to reconnect back with the cultivated olive tree.

Great warfare and strife comes in and kills revivals.

I believe that we should celebrate Messiah every day, even on Sunday (called in the Holy Scriptures the first day of the week), but Sunday or the first day is no substitute for Yah's holy Sabbath instituted at creation. That is creational law. The first thing that Constantine did through the Council of Nicaea was to disconnect the church from celebrating the biblical feasts, the Moadim, according to the original calculation of the Jews which is the biblical calculation that the Jews have preserved since Elohim gave it to Moses in Sinai. This is what Constantine wrote in the Council of Nicaea's document:

When the question relative to the sacred festival of Easter arose, it was universally thought that it would be convenient that all should keep the feast on one day; for what could be more beautiful and more desirable than to see this festival, through which we receive the hope of immortality, celebrated by all with one accord and in the same manner? It was declared to be particularly unworthy for this, the holiest of festivals to follow the customs (the calculation) of the Jews, *who had soiled their hands with the most fearful of crimes,* and whose minds were blinded. *In rejecting their custom,* we may transmit to our descendants the *legitimate* mode of celebrating Easter; which we have observed from the time of the Savior's passion (according to the day of the week).

We ought not therefore to have anything in common with the Jew, for the Savior has shown us another way; our worship following a more legitimate and more convenient course (the order of the days of the week): And consequently, in unanimously adopting this mode, we desire, dearest brethren to separate ourselves from the detestable company of the Jew for it is truly shameful for us to hear them boast that without their direction we could not keep this feast.

So, Constantine altered the times and removed the biblical calculations and customs from the church (the calculations and customs of the Jews). He also established that there is no need for the Jews to direct the church or to teach the Gentile Christians. Right after that, the church fell into a terrible apostasy. She began to kill Jews in the name of Christ! She began to celebrate pagan feasts such as Christmas, Halloween (witches' day) or the All Saints Day and Easter (from the Goddess of fertility Ishtar). She *replaced* the holy shabbat for the Sunday. She went ahead to claim that the laws of the Creator have changed and are actually abolished!

Soon after that, the Dark Ages set in, and then the Crusades and then the pogroms in Europe and Russia, and then the Spanish Inquisition, and then the Holocaust and *now*?

The Council of Nicaea instituted another gospel, but this gospel was no good news at all! The only way beloved, to be restored to the original gospel of the Kingdom is to get rid of the Council of Nicaea and of all replacement theologies, including feasts of pagan origin and return to honor the *Moadim*, the times and seasons and laws of the unchangeable, immutable, holy God of Israel, the Creator of heaven and earth who sits on His throne between the Cherubim and the Lamb who sits on the right hand of majesty. Yeshua would have never celebrated Christmas or Easter and He would never have replaced Shabbat for Sunday. He would have never violated the Word of His Father. He did not come to abolish or to violate the law and the prophets; He came to demonstrate it and to interpret it to the *full*. That is how He walked, and we, being His, are called to follow in His footsteps and walk even as He walked. (Matthew 5:17-20)

We see that the divorce from the olive tree and the alteration of times and laws caused the anti-Messiah to sit on the throne of Yeshua on earth, that is the church. The fruit of this, as history proves it, is disastrous! The church lost her glory, power and anointing and every time that there is a revival in order to restore it, that spirit of anti-Messiah causes havoc, strife and chaos and revivals stop. Remember that anti-Messiah is anti-anointing!

The only wise thing that we can do is repent, get rid of all Roman and pagan feasts as well as influence, and return to the holy seasons, to the holy Moadim of the ancient olive tree.

These altered seasons are like the leaves of the wild olive, they are unusable and the fruit that comes out of them is like the non-edible olives. We need to remember that it is these altered seasons that Satan has used in order to fill the church with the spirit of anti-Messiah. So, whoever decides to keep them saying that he is *free,* also decides to keep the spirit of the Antichrist himself!

I will never forget a beautiful church in Australia. When they heard the truth about replacement theology and Pagan Feasts, they responded so beautifully. I preached on a Saturday night and on the following Sunday they all brought their Christmas trees and Easter decorations in order to make a big fire and burn them. The glory of God was released in that church! As they came to the altar they were repenting and weeping as they placed these unholy decorations that they thought to be godly before. The Holy Spirit gave them deep conviction and they followed through.

I pray that the Holy Spirit gives everyone that reads this book deep conviction and that you follow through! In later chapters I will teach you about how to restore Shabbat and the holy feasts and Moadim to your life; but Yah does not like *mixture*. Go ahead and reject the pagan and the unholy and come be restored to the *Holy*. My husband, Baruch always jokes about it as he explains: You are only giving up so little and you will get back 9 festivals and some of them are seven and even eight days long! Whenever the devil deceives, he makes you think that he can offer so much more than the Creator, the great *I AM*; but he is a liar, and the father of all lies and was a liar from the beginning. We see this clearly in the Book of Genesis. No one can out-give the Most High. He is *good* and His mercy endures forever. His laws are *good*, His *times* and *feasts* are *good*, His ways are *all good* and *perfect* and the original cultivated olive tree is *good*!

"Hear the Word which Yahveh speaks to you, O house of Israel. Thus, says Yahveh, 'Do not learn the ways of the nations (Rome, Babylon) and do not be terrified by the signs of the heavens (horoscopes!), although the nations are terrified by them. For the customs of the peoples (Constantine) are delusion; because it is wood cut from the forest, the work of the hands of a craftsman with a cutting tool. They decorate it with silver and gold; they fasten it with a hammer that it will not topple (Christmas tree!)"

— Jeremiah 10:1-4

The Holy Word says that the customs of the nations are *delusional* and this is what the church inherited through Constantine: pagan traditions, pagan feasts and delusions.

Let us get rid of the delusions and move on to celebrate Yahveh's Holy Moadim!

Let Us Pray

Yes, Father! I repent for celebrating unholy feasts and harboring Babylonian-Roman traditions. Forgive me for my ignorance. From this day I follow through and will get rid and dispose of and burn all decorations or items connected with Constantine's feasts of Easter, Christmas or Halloween (witches' day). I give up the ways of the nations that are delusion and I learn the Hebrew biblical way. In Yeshua's holy name. Amen.

CHAPTER FOUR:

The Gospel of the Kingdom

"As He was sitting in the mount of olives, the disciples came to Him privately, saying, "Tell us, when will these things happen, and what will be the sign of Your coming, and of the end of the age? And Yeshua answered and said to them, "See that no one misleads you, for many will come in My name saying, 'I am the Messiah 'and will mislead many.' You will be hearing of wars and rumors of wars. See that you are not frightened, for those things must take place, but that is not yet the end. For nation will rise against nation, and Kingdom against Kingdom, and in various places there will be famines and earthquakes; but all these are merely the beginning of birth pangs. Then they will deliver you to tribulation, and will kill you, and you will be hated by all nations because of my name. At that time many will fall away and will betray one another and hate one another. Many false prophets will arise and will mislead many; because lawlessness is increased, most people's love will grow cold. But the one who endures to the end will be saved. This gospel of the Kingdom shall be preached in the whole world as a testimony to all the nations, and then the end will come."

— Matthew 24:3-14

his passage of Scripture describes very clearly what happened before and after the Council of Nicaea. Right before Emperor Constantine began to rule, there was a great persecution against the church. Many believers were fed to the lions in roman coliseums. Eventually, when the church adopted Constantine's Christian System another persecution arose and now it was the Gentile Christians against the Messianic Jews who refused to compromise with Constantine! Already before Constantine, Tertullian, St Augustine and other Gentile church fathers harbored terrible Anti-Jewish doctrines, and now those doctrines had been institutionalized. Everything Jewish, including the Hebrew Holy Scriptures, the Hebrew name of the Messiah, the biblical feasts, the Torah, etc., was outlawed. Those Messianic Jews that wanted to keep the original gospel of the Kingdom were expelled out of the church as heretics or even killed and betrayed by their own Christian brethren.

As the mixture of paganism entered the church and the spirit of anti-Messiah began to rule in it due to many false prophets and replacement theologians, it increased! (Torah and Yah's law was decreed obsolete; the Hebrew Holy Scriptures were renamed 'Old Testament' and the Apostolic writings were canonized as 'New Testament'). Due to the increase of lawlessness, iniquity and sin in the 'Mixed Church', the love of many grew so cold as to turn the church into another entity. It did not resemble the early church in anything! Those that tried to keep their faith during that time had to endure much persecution. Some endured but many were lost. Romans 11:17-22 warned us that this could happen.

"...But if some of the branches were broken off and you, being a wild olive, were grafted in among them and became partaker with them of the rich root of the olive tree, *do not be arrogant against the branches;* but if you are remembered that it is not you who supports the root, but the root supports you. You will say then, 'Branches were broken off so that I might be grafted in. Quite right, they were broken off for their unbelief, but you stand by your faith. *Do not be conceited but fear; for if God did not spare the natural branches, He will not spare you either.* Behold the kindness and the severity of God; to those who fell severity, but to you God's kindness, *if you continue in His kindness; otherwise you also will be cut off."*

Sadly, we have lost many Gentile branches that have been cut off because of arrogance against the Jews and as they fell prey to replacement theology and to the spirit of anti-Messiah; but now in the third millennium we need to rise up and rescue the church from this deception! Even today as we travel throughout many nations, I notice that the church is suffering from lawlessness, and iniquity, being lukewarm and in immorality—and many preachers are still preaching replacement theology. Every place that we go to, people share with us about immoral pastors, adulterous leaders that delve into pornography and the like. It looks like a plague of iniquity is in the church and the love of many is growing colder and colder.

So, what is the answer to this extremely dangerous condition? Repentance from lawlessness that comes from hearing the wrong gospel! The gospel mixed with replacement theology is not the true gospel. A gospel that does not preach holiness and repentance is a false gospel. The good news of the Kingdom is exactly that. It is *good news* and it is about a *Kingdom*, the *Kingdom of God*! That Kingdom comes with power and it also has laws. A gospel that says that the law is done away with, and that a Christian is 'free' from it, is a heresy! It has created a lot of mixed, confused and unholy people, who are constantly struggling with the same sins and have no power or victory in their lives. They are so used to the 'mixture' that they think it's normal. No, it is not normal— this false gospel is coming from Constantine's time, and it's time to expose it and get rid of it.

My purpose for writing this book and the truth is so that you can be free! Then you can go into greatness and be an effective vessel in the hands of the Most High; but the Word says that in order to be free, we need to know the truth intimately (John 8:32). The truth is Yeshua Himself, and He is very jealous for His bride, for you! He will not share or commune with lies or with false gospels or replacement theologies. He wants your heart clean from all lies and lying doctrines, so He can write the gospel of the Kingdom in your heart. Then He will anoint that gospel and will use you mightily to turn the world around like the Jewish disciples 2000 years ago. But for that we have to be restored to the same gospel they preached and to the foundations that they stood on.

Those foundations are not Christian; they are Jewish, Hebrew, and biblically Jewish. None of the Jewish Apostles were Christians.

They were Jews and they were disciples. They were people of the Way! Today the word Christian doesn't necessarily mean a disciple. It only means a certain religious persuasion, such as Moslem or Buddhist.

The gospel of the Kingdom does not make Christians. It makes on fire holy disciples, empowered by the power of the Holy Spirit, walking in greatness and in the glory of YHVH. The gospel of the Kingdom tolerates *no mixture* and no deception. A gospel that does not create holy, on fire, obedient disciples is not the gospel of the Kingdom, it is another gospel! As I move through the body of Messiah today, very seldom do I meet a true disciple or even a true man or woman of God. Most Christians have a lot of hidden sin, both in their minds, hearts and lives. I do not see a holy, on fire church that causes the heathen to be afraid of her. So the gospel of the Kingdom is not being preached in most places, only a compromised gospel is being preached.

"At the hands of the apostles many signs and wonders were taking place among the people; and they were all with one accord in Solomon's portico; but none of the rest dared to associate with them; however, the people held them in high esteem. And all the more believers in the Lord, multitudes of men and women, were constantly added to their

number, to such an extent that they even carried the sick out into the streets and laid them on cots and pallets, so that when Peter came by, at least his shadow might fall on any one of them. Also, the people from the cities in the vicinity of Jerusalem were coming together; bringing people who were sick or afflicted with unclean spirits, and they were all being healed."

— Acts 5:12-15

This awesome revival followed the event described in Acts 5, when a Jewish couple, Ananias and Saphiras, lied about an offering that they had promised. As they lied to Peter, he said, that 'they had lied to the Holy Spirit' and immediately first the man and then the wife dropped dead! They dropped dead because of lying, because they broke Yah's ninth Commandment (Deuteronomy 5:20). When the true gospel is being preached, sin is not tolerated; the breaking of God's Commandments is not acceptable anymore – not even with new believers!

So many times, I hear people and pastors justifying unholy behavior in people by saying, 'Well you know, she or he is a new believer!' That is not the way that the Apostles thought. I am sure that Ananias and Saphiras were fairly new believers, since the whole movement was new. And what about the way that Peter dealt with Simon the sorcerer a moment after his water baptism?

"Even Simon himself believed; and after being baptized, he continued on with Philip, and as he observed signs and great miracles taking place, he was constantly amazed."

— Acts 8:13

This Simon had been a sorcerer and he was accustomed to witchcraft signs and wonders, he had worked with the dark powers; but here we see him as a 'new babe' freshly baptized, without undergoing any extensive new believers' class like in most churches! He was following the evangelist around and learning by watching. The miracles that he was seeing were not little headaches being cured. They were true miracles that left him astounded!

"Now when the apostles in Jerusalem heard that Samaria had received the Word of God, they sent for Peter and John, who came down and prayed for them that they might receive the Holy Spirit. Then they began laying their hands on them, and they were receiving the Holy Spirit. Now when Simon (the new 'baby believer') saw that the Spirit was bestowed through the laying on of the apostle's hands, he offered them money. Saying, 'Give this authority to me that everyone on whom I lay my hands may receive the Holy Spirit. But Peter said to him, 'May your silver perish with you, because you thought that you could obtain the gift of God with money! You have no part or portion in this matter, for your heart is not right before God! Therefore, repent of this wickedness of yours and pray the Lord that if possible, the intention

of your heart may be forgiven you. For I see that you are in the gall of bitterness and in the bondage of iniquity."

— Acts 8:14-23

Simon was so scared after Peter's harsh rebuke that he answered:

"Pray to the Lord for me yourselves, so that nothing of what you have said may come upon me."

— Acts 8:24

When is the last time that you heard that someone dropped dead in the church because of lying about an offering? Or that a pastor rebuked a new believer who is still bound into witchcraft and immorality without justifying his sin but calling him to accountability for it? Most modern-day pastors do not have the anointing or the authority to truly correct sin, because they themselves harbor it in their heart. This false gospel that has been preached since the church divorced from its Apostolic Jewish foundation has to be renounced and true holiness must be restored! Then and only then there will be an End time Apostolic church that will make the Jews jealous and move in signs and wonders and miracles. A church that can turn around the nations. The key is to renounce the Council of Nicaea, Babylonian Christianity with its unholy feasts, accept Yeshua as a *Jew* and get re-grafted back into the cultivated olive tree.

When Paul walked and preached the true gospel of the Kingdom, strange things happened to him. Most preachers today would not be willing to suffer what Rabbi Saul, Paul the Apostle suffered when he walked an uncompromised holy gospel.

Paul walked in obedience to Yah's Commandments, as his Master Yeshua the Messiah did before him. He honored the laws of God and they were written in his heart. He walked a holy walk and the Spirit of grace worked mightily through him and through Timothy and Priscilla and Aquilla and Apollos and Lydia! Many of the writings of Paul have been misinterpreted through Gentile replacement theologians. It is time to hear some Jewish End time Apostles reinterpret Paul. It is time that the Holy Spirit writes His law in our hearts which is the mark of the true new covenant. (Jeremiah 31:31-34)

It is time to go back to the true gospel of the Kingdom, followed with astounding signs, wonders and miracles. This gospel will be preached again by a holy church that is totally grafted in! Will you be a part of it?

"This gospel of the Kingdom shall be preached in the whole world as a testimony to all the nations, and then the end will come."

— Matthew 24:14

CHAPTER FIVE:

Keep the Shabbat Holy

"So, the Sons of Israel shall observe the Sabbath, to celebrate the Sabbath throughout their generations as a perpetual covenant. It is a sign between me and the Sons of Israel forever; for in six days Yahveh made the heavens and the earth, but on the seventh day He ceased from labor, and was refreshed."

— Exodus 31:16, 17

The restoration of the holy times and seasons is one of the marks of the End times glorious church. Since the mark of the anti-Messiah was the alteration of the times, the task of the Messianic or Anointed church is to restore the seasons and the testimonials, the Moadim of Yahveh and they begin with the shabbat, called the Sabbath in the English translations. The *shabbat* is the number one testimonial or holy convocation and it comes around *every* week from Friday sundown to Saturday sundown. Remember what I explained in a former chapter about *Moadim* or *testimonials*, Yah's holy seasons and timings? That it is the appointed time that He demonstrates Himself and 'shows up.' By removing them the church lost a lot of power, revelation and anointing. Let me explain this in another way. Let us say that a woman is married and has a wonderful husband.

Now that husband has told her that he desires to keep the marriage fresh and exciting and very intimate. Therefore, in order to do so it is very important to separate special times to date each other. Those dates would be consistent, so that no matter what happened and how hectic life might become, they would always put those dates first and give them priority. Those dating times would be their very special secret, the token and the sign of their love. Can you imagine what would happen in that husband's heart if every time the date came around, he would come to meet his wife, desirous to share his best with her, but she would be missing? Not only that but she would actually speak against those dating times and say that they are obsolete and abolished and belong to the past?

This is actually what happened to the church through replacement theology. Shabbat became not only a thing of the past, but it became forbidden. During the Middle Ages when Jews tried to escape the persecution against them by the church of that time, they had to *publicly* renounce the celebration and the keeping of the shabbat and the holy feasts of Yahveh. The following is an excerpt from a typical profession of faith that a Jewish baptismal candidate was forced to confess. (Taken from holy to Yahveh by Terry Goldblum Seedman, page 95)

"I do here and now renounce every rite and observance of the Jewish religion, detesting all its most solemn ceremonies...in the future I will practice no rite or celebration connected with it... promising neither to seek it out nor perform it...I promise that I will never return to the vomit of Jewish superstition. Never again will I fulfill any of the offices of Jewish ceremonies to which I was addicted, nor even hold them dear. I will shun all intercourse with other Jews and have the circle of my friends only among other Christians. We will not associate with the accursed Jews who remain un-baptized... We will not practice carnal circumcision, or celebrate the Passover, the Sabbath or the other feast days connected with the Jewish religion.

I renounce the whole worship of the Hebrews...And I absolutely renounce every custom and institution of the Jewish laws...In one word I renounce everything Jewish... If I wander from the straight path in any way and defile the Holy Faith, and try to observe any rites of the Jewish sect, or if I should delude you in any way in the swearing of this oath...then may all the curses of the law fall upon me...may there fall upon me and upon my house and all my children all the plagues that smote Egypt..." And on, and on...

So, in order to become a Christian, a Jew had to renounce the Hebrew holy Scriptures, the laws of Yahveh and the celebration of the Shabbat and His holy feasts: "

Yahveh spoke to Moses saying, "speak to the Sons of Israel and say to them, Yahveh's appointed times which you shall proclaim as Holy convocations—*My appointed times are these:* For six days you shall work, but on the seventh day there is a Sabbath of complete rest, a Holy convocation. You shall not do any work; it is a Sabbath to Yahveh in all your dwellings."

— Leviticus 23:1-3

Please note that these feasts, beginning with the Shabbat are His holy feasts and He says that the Shabbat is to Yahveh. In the Scripture that opens this chapter from Exodus 31:16, it says that the Shabbat is a *perpetual covenant* and a *sign forever*. When the devil, through replacement theology in Christianity tried to remove that sign from the Jewish people, he was trying to declare God a liar! Because, if the Jews do not honor the Shabbat any longer, then it is not a sign forever, neither a perpetual covenant. There is a Jewish saying that describes the importance of the Shabbat in order to be blessed: "More than the Jews kept the Shabbat, the Shabbat kept the Jews."

We could argue the point here that this is a sign between Yah and Israel only, so the Gentiles who are grafted in should not celebrate it; or perhaps to the Christians, God gave the Sunday. Let us test these arguments.

In chapter one we talked about being grafted in and what it meant. Among other things it meant sharing the same biblical culture.

"...But if some of the branches were broken off and you, being a wild olive, *were grafted in among them and became partakers with them of the rich root of the olive tree*, do not be arrogant against the branches; but if you are, remember that it is not you who supports the root, *but the root supports you.*"

— Romans 11:17, 18

1. Shabbat is not a tradition, it is a Commandment, and it is the fourth of the Ten Commandments. Later on in Chapter Seven we will learn the importance of these 10 laws.

"Observe the Sabbath day to keep it Holy as Yahveh Elohim has commanded you. Six days you shall labor and do all your work, but the seventh day is the Sabbath of Yahveh your Elohim."

— Deuteronomy 5:12-14

2. The Shabbat is a Creational Commandment and is one of the Ten Commandments. Elohim separates the seventh day as holy already at creation.

"By the seventh day God completed His work which He had done, and He rested on the seventh day from all the work which He had done.

Then God blessed the seventh day and sanctified it, because in it He rested from all His work which God had created and made."

3. Gentiles coming to the covenant are required to honor Yahveh's laws including the Shabbat. *"Also,* the foreigners *who join themselves to Yahveh, to minister to Him, and to love the name of Yahveh, to be His servants,* everyone who keeps from profaning the Sabbath *and holds fast my covenant; Even those I will bring to my Holy mountain and make them joyful in my house of prayer. For my house will be called a house of prayer for all the peoples."*

4. The Shabbat will be celebrated and honored for all eternity by all nations.

"For just as the new heavens and the new earth which I make will endure before me, declares Yahveh, so your offspring and your name will endure. It shall be that from new moon to new moon and *from Sabbath to Sabbath all mankind will come* to bow down before Me says Yahveh."

— Isaiah 66:22-23

5. There is not one Scripture that states that God changed the Shabbat to Sunday. *"For I AM Yahveh; I change not" "Forever O Yahveh Your Word is settled in heaven."* (Malachi 3:1, Psalms 119:89)

6. Sunday worship was instituted by Constantine after the Council of Nicea as a state law because that was the day

that he worshipped the sun. That is why it is called Sunday. As part of the system of replacement theology, its purpose was to replace Yahveh's Holy Day. Yeshua called Himself the Lord of the Shabbat. *"For the Son of man is Lord even of the Sabbath day."* In other words, He is the owner of this day and no one can exchange it. However, the way of keeping it may vary at different times and in different cultures (please see Chapter Eight on "Practical Life Applications").

Let Us Bow Down Our Heads and Pray

Dear Father in heaven, I realize that out of ignorance I have broken Your fourth Commandment by not keeping the Shabbat holy. I ask for Your forgiveness and for Your cleansing from this unrighteousness. I also ask forgiveness for the Christians that throughout history have rejected this Commandment and have even forced Jews to break it. I realize that this is a great sin and I ask for mercy now. Please teach me and all the church how to keep Your Shabbat holy and help me to teach others also. In Yeshua's name. Amen.

Restoring the Shabbat

First of all, let us take a look at this marvelous promise,

"If because of the Shabbat, you turn your foot from doing your own pleasure on My Holy day, and call the Sabbath a delight, the Holy day of Yahveh honorable, and honor it, desisting from your own ways, from seeking your own pleasure and speaking your own word. Then you will

take delight in Yahveh, and I will make you ride on the heights of the earth; and I will feed you with the heritage of Jacob your father, for the mouth of Yahveh has spoken."

— Isaiah 58:13, 14

We again see here that the Shabbat is Yah's holy day. We also see a connection between the blessing and between keeping the Shabbat holy. He promises to make us ride on the heights, in other words to be the head and not the tail. He also promises to feed us with the inheritance of our father Jacob. In other words—with the blessing of Abraham as Jacob inherited the blessing from Isaac who inherited it from Abraham. Let us see what this blessing is:

"...And I will make you a great nation, and I will bless you, and make your name great; and so you shall be a blessing; and I will bless those who bless you, and the one who curses you I will curse. And in you all the families of the earth will be blessed."

— Genesis 12:2, 3

Let us see if this is consistent with the words of Yeshua:

"Do not think that I have come to abolish the law or the prophets; I did not come to abolish but to fulfill. For truly I say to you, until heaven and earth pass away, not the smallest letter or stroke shall pass from the Law until all is accomplished. Whoever then annuls one of the least of these Commandments, and teaches others to do the same, shall be

called least in the Kingdom of heaven; but whoever keeps and teaches them shall be called great in the Kingdom of heaven."

— Matthew 5:17-19

The Shabbat is not one of the least of the Commandments, but rather one of the most important ones and that is why the enemy has sought to remove it from the Jews and from the church! As we begin to keep the Shabbat holy and to celebrate it, we will begin to see marks of greatness in our lives and will enter into a new dimension of the Blessing of Abraham.

You may hear people argue that Paul was against keeping the Shabbat and in fact warned against it. Let me tell you that Paul has been seriously misinterpreted since the church divorced from its Jewish roots! Replacement theologians have literally 'butchered' Paul's writings. First of all, Paul cannot contradict Yeshua, otherwise he would be in rebellion against the Messiah Himself. So, whatever Paul said that sounds like a contradiction to Yeshua's words, needs to be reinterpreted. This is the principle.

Paul loved the law, the Torah, but hated legalism! He was not against the law; otherwise, he would have been labeled a heretic and a lawless one. He was against the spirit of legalism!

The following are also the words of Paul,

"So then the Law is Holy, and the Commandment is Holy, righteous and good. Therefore, did that which is good become a cause of death for me? May it never be! Rather it was sin..."

— Romans 7:12, 13

Paul himself kept the law and the Shabbat holy; he even honored the Jewish traditions.

"After three days Paul called together those who were leading men of the Jews, and when they came together, he began saying to them, "Brethren, though I had done nothing against our people or the customs of our fathers, yet I was delivered as a prisoner from Jerusalem into the hands of the Romans."

— Romans 28:17

Was Paul lying in order to get out of trouble with the Jews? God forbids! He was telling the absolute truth. The Jewish Rabbi, Apostle to the Gentiles, walked in obedience to the Torah laws, including the Shabbat all the days of his life—just like his Master Yeshua did.

Let us take a look at the following Scripture:

"And on the Sabbath day we went outside the gate to a riverside, where we were supposing there would be a place of prayer; and we sat down and began speaking to the women who had assembled."

— Acts 16:13

When Paul was traveling in his apostolic journeys, he kept the Shabbat holy and so did all of his apostolic team.

That is why they were looking for a place of prayer outside of a pagan city, away from the noise of the merchants. Do you suppose that there were some Gentile believers in Paul's apostolic team? Of course, there were, but since there was no question that they were grafted into the olive tree, there was no question that they too walked in obedience to the laws of the covenant and kept the Shabbat holy!

In the following chapters I will teach you how to walk in obedience to the Commandments and how to discern their level of importance. You will understand how to please Yah without any ounce of legalism but completely walking in the Holy Spirit. You will see that the Father's intentions had been all the time that His laws would dwell in your heart richly and that you would be blessed with the blessing of Abraham!

"For all who are being led by the Spirit of God these are the Sons of God."

— Romans 8:14

CHAPTER SIX:

Grace and Law

"Mercy and truth have met together; righteousness and peace have kissed each other."

— Psalm 85:10

In the garden of Eden there were many trees, however two trees were very prominent; one was the tree of knowledge of good and evil and the other one was the tree of life. Eating the fruit of the first always brings death and eating the fruit of the second brings abundant and eternal life. Elohim wanted Adam to eat of the tree of life and live forever in His blessing and presence; but Adam chose the 'knowledge of good and evil' rather than the life. The poison of that tree is so deathly, that it prevents people from going into life. They eat and are dying with every bite, but they think that it is good and holy! (Genesis 2:8-17)

Some time ago I was in a prominent city in the USA and a local leader, a TV personality, said approximately these words in the middle of his preaching;

"If God did not want Adam to eat of the tree of knowledge, He would have not put it in the Garden of Eden! Elohim was not forbidding Adam to eat of it as an absolute law; He wanted Adam to be mature enough so he could 'handle' the knowledge of good and evil!"

What this preacher was saying, is that God is not a God of absolutes. His no is not *no*, and His yes is not *yes*! He is an ambivalent God. In other words, His Word has a hidden meaning that is only for the 'wise and for the mature.' This is exactly what advocates of Kabala, Freemasonry and other secret cults and religions claim. *"In order to know the depth of truth one has to be 'mature' or 'old enough', advanced enough, etc."* This is the mark of every deceptive theology; there is one truth for the 'inexperienced' and another 'deeper truth' for the mature.

Let us see what the Word has to say about this:

"The secret things belong to Yahveh our Creator, but the things revealed belong to us and to our Sons, forever, that we may observe all the words of this law."

— Deuteronomy 29:29

Yahveh's revelation belongs to *both* adults and children, to the point that *both* adults and children are empowered equally to obey Yah's Commandments.

"At that time Yeshua said, "I praise you Father, Lord of heaven and earth, that You have hidden these things from the wise and intelligent and have revealed them to infants."

— Matthew 11:25

Contrary to all other religions, sects, cults and secret societies, the *truth* of Elohim is revealed unto *babies*, unto *infants*! Yet religion makes everything very complicated. There are hundreds of theological volumes that have been written to support the lie of "replacement theology" and the "Cheap grace 'gospel'." You have to be extremely 'intellectual' and a 'real scholar' to understand the intense theological debates about it. It is so confusing that most people give up altogether and do not understand what they believe in. Another word for confusion is "Babylon."

"...And He called a child to Himself and set him before them, and said, "Truly I say to you, unless you are converted and become like children, you will not enter the Kingdom of heaven."

— Matthew 18:2, 3

That sums it all up! I believe that most of the church needs to go through conversion to become like little children again and receive the gospel of the Kingdom as it was delivered by the Jewish Apostles prior to the Council of Nicaea.

"For consider your calling brethren, that there were not many wise according to the flesh, not many mighty, not many noble; But God has chosen the foolish things of this world to shame the wise, and God has chosen the weak things of the world to shame the things which are strong."

— 1 Corinthians 1:26, 27

One day the Father told me, *"Dominiquae, I did not call theologians to govern My Body and to teach doctrine. I have chosen APOSTLES!"*

'Now, as they observed the confidence of Peter and John and understood that they were uneducated and untrained men, they were amazed, and began to recognize them as having been with Yeshua."

— Acts 4:13

The theologians of that time recognized that Peter and John had not been 'theologically educated.' They had not learnt any homiletics or hermeneutics. They had not been to rabbinical school, but they had been with *the rabbi*! They had spent three and a half years with the Word, the Torah, and the law made flesh. It is about time that we spent some time with our Jewish Rabbi, the Lion of Judah and sat on His knees to learn Torah, to study His Commandments and promises. This is why it is a matter of life and death to be *filled* with the Spirit; because He is our Torah teacher, He is our Rabbi. You do not need theological books to help you understand His Word; you need the Holy Spirit! You need to reject the fruit of the tree of the knowledge of good and evil, that is the fruit of replacement theology and of 'Babylonian Christianity.' It is so confusing, so complicated that most people don't understand what they believe in. So, in order to be 'like everyone else,' they compromise the still small voice of the Holy Spirit that desires to teach them *truth*.

The Truth Is Very Simple to Understand!

"Mercy and truth have met together; righteousness and peace have kissed each other."

— Psalm 85:10

This verse explains it so clearly.

Mercy is the word *chesed* in Hebrew, which is one of the forms of saying "grace." "Truth" is the word *emet* in Hebrew as used in Psalm 119:142, "Your righteousness is an everlasting righteousness, and Your law is *truth*." Later on Yeshua would say: "I AM the way, and the truth and the life; no one comes to the Father but through Me." Let me paraphrase what Yeshua was saying:

"I AM the character of God (the way), and the law of God (the truth) and the power of God (the life), no one comes to the Father unless he comes through ALL of Me!"

All of Him
- The Character of Yah
- The Law of Yah
- The Power of Yah

There have been so many futile debates in the church because of the confusion of the Babylonian spirit about what is the right doctrine. Are tongues for today, is healing for today, is love the only gift or are the gifts of the Spirit for today still? Is the law for today, or is it only grace with no law? Is holy laughter for today, are apostles for today, or only pastors? Do bishops still exist or are they extinct? Is the Shabbat for today? Is prosperity for today, or is it poverty? Are we under the law or under grace? And the arguments go on and on.

I will never forget when we were in a city in Peru and were ministering at an evangelical home meeting. As I shared about Yeshua being a Jew, the Holy Spirit (as He does in most of our meetings) began to confirm the message of the true gospel with signs, wonders and miracles! I received a 'word of knowledge 'about some sickness, and as I shared, people began to receive divine healing. As people were getting healed, one of the ladies (who had received miraculous healing in front of everyone) kept on arguing that the gifts of the Holy Spirit (1 Corinthians 12) are not important today because we have the giver of the gifts. Who said that we needed to choose the giver or His gifts? We need to have the giver (Yeshua) with His gifts!

It was quite a sight as she was arguing vehemently, in the midst of receiving healing to her damaged back! As I confronted the lies that she had believed, she finally humbled her heart enough to listen. On that night, most people present were healed, and a deathly doctrine was confronted. Dear people, deceptive doctrines are an evil spirit that feeds you of the tree of knowledge of good and evil and not the tree of life. This spirit needs to be cast out and your spiritual food has to change!

In the true New Covenant, the law is written in the heart! (Jeremiah 31:31-34) We do not have to choose between grace and law, we need them *both!* We need the mercy, the *chesed* and we need the truth, the *emet*. We need the way, the truth and the life! We need the Word and we need the Spirit! We cannot do anything without His power, His Spirit. But His Spirit works with His Word, with His laws and Commandments and writes His ways and laws in our heart. This is a simple truth that many theologians cannot understand but any simple babe in the faith can:

The law is not done away with; Yeshua is not done away with. It only changes location; instead of being written on tablets of stone is the law is now written in hearts of flesh by the Holy Spirit. Yeshua is also the Torah, the law made flesh, and through Him we know how to walk in obedience to the Father!

Mercy and truth have met in Yeshua and His grace has transported us from the Kingdom of darkness, sin, lawlessness and rebellion to the Kingdom of light, righteousness, law and obedience. His Kingdom is manifested in our hearts made flesh. Our hearts become the writing pad of the Holy Spirit who is the finger of God!

An Important Prayer

Dear Father in heaven, please forgive me for any pride in my heart and for any confusion or Babylon in my mind. I know that You are not an author of confusion but of order! I humble my heart and convert to become like a little child again. Please reveal to me the truth of Your Word and Commandments. I receive *all* of You, the way, the truth and the life. I receive Your grace and Your law, Your Word and Your Spirit, the fruits of the Spirit and the gifts of the Spirit. I totally reject the fruit of religion that comes from the tree of knowledge of good and evil. I begin to eat of the Tree of Life! In Yeshua's name. Amen.

"He who has an ear let him ear what the Spirit says to the churches, to him who overcomes, I will grant to eat of the tree of life which is in the paradise of God."

— Revelation 2:7

Let us keep on eating Paradise's fruit!

CHAPTER SEVEN:

The Knowledge of the Glory

"For the earth will be filled with the knowledge of the glory of Yahveh, as the waters cover the sea."

— Habakkuk 2:14

What a marvelous promise! But how will this promise to come to pass? Nowadays as we look on the world and its condition, we are far from seeing the glory of God covering the earth! I would say that the earth is on the verge of turning like Sodom and Gomorra. Sin is rampart everywhere, divorce rates are increasing, poverty, and immorality and idolatry seem to be covering the earth right now. Waves of terrorism, violence and kidnappings seem to be the order of the day. So, is this Scripture a utopia, a fantasy, or a nice fairy tale? And if it is true, when will it come to pass? Is it possible to change the world situation from the 'knowledge of darkness and Satan' that seems to be prevailing, to the knowledge of the glory of God?

My answer is an emphatic yes! However, we need to answer the calling given by Yeshua to the Jewish disciples and through them to the Gentile believers 2000 years ago in Matthew 28,

"And Yeshua came up and spoke to them, saying all authority has been given to Me in heaven and on earth. Go therefore and make disciples of all the nations, baptizing them in the name of the Father, the Son and the Holy Spirit,[5] teaching them to observe all that I commanded you; and lo I am with you always, even to the End of the age."

— Matthew 28:18-19

No one will use a 'magic wand' to change the world's condition from sin and wickedness to the knowledge of the glory of Yahveh. The way that this will happen will be by obeying the Great Commission. However, even the great commission has been greatly misinterpreted since the Council of Nicea, just like the true gospel of the Kingdom has been. So, what is the great commission that is the *key* to fill the earth with the knowledge of the glory of God just like the waters cover the sea?

---

5   Some scholars believe that the original text (that used to be in Eusebius library in Caesarea) probably said, "Baptizing them in my name", which would be consistent with the entire Book of Acts, where people are baptized into the Name of Yeshua. This is into His death, burial and resurrection.

1. Using the authority given by Yeshua to heal the sick, cast out devils, raise the dead, etc. (Mark 16-16)
2. To make disciples of all nations by teaching them God's ways!
3. Teaching them to obey God's Commandments this is the plan and there is no other!

When is the last time that you heard the Commandments of Yah taught in a church service or on TV? How many nations has the church made into disciples? It says *of* all nations, in other words the church has to *disciple*, not only evangelize nations. But how can she disciple, if she herself is a 'backsliding, lukewarm Christian and not a disciple?' How can she teach the world God's Commandments if she herself is not honoring them and her preachers preach that the law is done away with? That we are now in the 'dispensation of grace', so breaking God's Commandments carries no consequences because He is 'merciful.' And if the breaking of Yah's laws carries no consequences, how come that the lives of many Christians are still filled with so many marks of the curse rather than the blessing? And how come that the church in its entirety is not yet glorified, prosperous, and influential? Where are the marks of God's favor?

I was in a certain Latin American country a while ago and after two days of preaching there (this was my third time in that country), I was disgusted with the offerings that I was receiving. It was an offence to the glory of God! The people there were poor, but one of the reasons for their poverty was their lack of correct giving.

Later on, we will touch on this very important subject, and you will learn that the Father does not receive just any offering that we give Him. (See Genesis four, how He refused Cain's offering, and see Malachi chapter one).

I was complaining before my Father, who is also my employer, as I preach the gospel and live off the gospel as prescribed. I will never forget what He told me. He woke me up the following morning, reprimanding me.

He said, *"How do you want this situation to change if you are not teaching them about Holy giving? If you will not put the right foundation how will they know? If you don't do it, who will?"* In other words, how do you want the knowledge of the glory to be in this nation if you do not obey the great commission which includes teaching them to observe or obey My Commandments?

To change the conditions of the nation's we have to use Yeshua's authority to heal the sick, deliver them from demons and also teach the people to obey Yah's Commandments! Then entire nations will become disciples!

We can see that every time that Israel kept Yahveh's Covenant, Israel was the head of the nations and was blessed. Every time that the kings and the priests taught the Commandments and pulled down the altars of Baal and Ashera and restored the work of the temple and the service of the Levites, they were blessed beyond description! Every time that she sinned and went into apostasy, she was given into the hands of her enemies; but the false gospel that has been taught since the Council of Nicea has caused people to think that the laws of the Almighty are not for today and that they are changed. That is why the Book of the Torah (Laws and instructions in righteousness) is called the "Old Testament."

In a previous chapter we saw that the spirit of anti-Messiah works through the removal of the Judaism of Messiah. That includes the Torah, since the most intricate part of being Jewish, is the Torah. Israel is the only nation in the world that God separated for Himself and to whom He gave Commandments. When the temple was in Jerusalem, many kings and people from other nations used to come to it to worship God and inquire of Him.

They came because they saw the *greatness* of Israel:

"For what great nation is there that has a God so near to it as Yahveh our Elohim whenever we call on Him? Or what great nation is there that has statutes and judgments as righteous as this whole law which I am setting before you today?"

— Deuteronomy 4:8

Is this done away with in the New Covenant? Look what Yeshua Himself said:

"Do not think that I have come to abolish the law or the prophets; I did not come to abolish but to fulfill. For truly I say to you, until heaven and earth pass away, not the smallest letter or stroke shall pass from the Law until all is accomplished. Whoever then annuls one of the least of these Commandments, and teaches others to do the same, shall be

called least in the Kingdom of heaven; *but whoever keeps and teaches them shall be called great in the Kingdom of heaven.*"

— Matthew 5:17-19

Yeshua warned us *not to even think* that He came to abolish the Torah, the law! Why do so many preachers preach against the Word of the Master Himself, misinterpreting Paul's words and exalting them above the words of Yeshua? The answer is very simple—because they have been fed replacement theology themselves and they do not know any better. However, the fruit of this false teaching is very obvious. Most Christians are struggling with sin constantly, pastors included. There is a raging battle inside of them between the Spirit of truth and replacement theology, which is a deceptive spirit. Every time that people renounce it and allow for the law to be written in their hearts by the Holy Spirit, deliverance, healing and peace come, and in due time their lives are completely restored.

Replacement theology is the main obstruction to the knowledge of the glory of Yahveh. Once it is out of our lives, teachings, doctrines and churches, we will be able to advance the Kingdom of God on earth faster than ever before.

Some time ago I was in Venezuela, and on the way to the airport the dear brother who was driving us was praying and worshiping the Father. He was thanking him for bringing us to bless his country. Since I detected a real hunger for truth in this precious man, I blessed him with the revelation of 'being grafted in.' As he received it and renounced the Council of

Nicaea and Babylonian Christianity, and accepted Yeshua as a Jewish Messiah into his heart, he was delivered. He described it like this:

"When I was praying this prayer, I saw the hand of God removing out of me a spirit and putting in me ANOTHER spirit. Then I saw that my heart was full of cement (hardness), and as the new spirit came in, the cement of my heart fell, and my heart became a heart of flesh!"

As he shared this testimony, his face had been transformed and he was shining! The knowledge of the glory had entered his heart, and now his heart was soft enough for the right Spirit, the Spirit of truth to write His laws in it without the obstruction of the *other* deceptive spirit of replacement theology.

Dear people, we see this happening all over the world! Every time that people pray that prayer with us, (sometimes entire meeting halls filled with thousands of people), their faces change, and they begin to *glow*! The knowledge of the glory comes into their hearts, the deceptive replacement theology spirit leaves; the Spirit of truth comes in and begins to write the Torah in their hearts. They all report a big transformation, peace, joy, and purity restored! In many cases instant miracles and healings take place as well, instant family reconciliations included! The fruit is *so tasty* and *so consistent.*

It is like finding the gold that people have been looking for, except this is gold refined in the fire of His presence! To confirm this, in many of our meetings we find gold glory dust all over the altar and many times it appears on the faces of many people or in their hands, clothes, etc. This is an End time sign calling the church to the glory of God, to buy gold refined in the fire!

This is what Yeshua said to the lukewarm church of Laodicea,

"I advise you to buy from Me gold refined by fire so that you may become rich, and white garments so that you may clothe yourself, and that the shame of your nakedness will not be revealed; and eye salve to anoint your eyes so you may see."

— Revelation 3:1

Replacement theology with its pagan feasts, Jew and Torah hatred, has left the church poor, naked and blind and yet great portions of it think that they are rich! In some areas the church looks so good, and they have such a great show going on. However, when you look into the lives of people and leadership alike, you see that hidden sin is rampant and they are all lukewarm.

"I know your deeds that you are neither cold nor hot; I wish that you were cold or hot. So, because you are lukewarm and neither hot nor cold, I will spit you out of my mouth. Because you say I am rich and have become wealthy and have need of nothing, and you do not know that you are wretched and miserable and poor and blind and naked, I advise you to buy of Me gold refined in the fire..."

— Revelation 3:15-18

The false replacement theology gospel has given a license to disrespect, disregard and break God's Commandments under the guise of "Grace." Yes, the Father is merciful, but He does not wink at sin. The wages of sin is death.

"What shall we say then? Are we to continue in sin so that grace may increase? May it never be! How shall we who died to sin still live in it? Or do you not know that all of us who have been baptized into Messiah Yeshua have been baptized into His death, so that as Messiah was raised from the dead through the glory of the Father, so we too might walk in the newness of life...Knowing this, that our old self was crucified with Him, in order that our body of sin might be done away with, so that we would no longer be slaves to sin."

— Romans 6:1-6

But What is Sin?

The Hebrew word for "sin" is *chet*, which means "to miss the target." It is likened unto an arrow that is shot off course and it deviates from its goal. The first time that sins appear on the earth is when the woman listens to Satan in the snake and she believes his lies. She goes ahead to break Elohim's Commandment to man,

"Elohim commanded the man saying, "From any tree of the garden you may eat freely; but from the tree of knowledge of good and evil you shall not eat, for in the day that you eat from it you shall surely die."

— Genesis 2:16, 17

When the snake tempted the woman, it enticed her to break God's Commandment, convincing her that it would not carry the terrible consequences that Elohim had said,

"Now the serpent was more crafty than any other beasts of the field which Yahveh Elohim had made. And he said to the woman, "Indeed has Elohim said, 'You shall not eat from any tree of the garden'? The woman said to the serpent, "From the fruit of the trees of the garden we may eat, but from the fruit of the tree, which is in the middle of the garden, Elohim has said, 'You shall not eat from it or touch it or you will die. 'The serpent said to the woman, 'You surely will not die! For Elohim knows that in the day you eat from it your eyes will be opened, and you will be like the Creator knowing good and evil."

— Genesis 3:1-5

What was the outcome? Adam and his wife lost the presence and the knowledge of the glory of God and they were cast out from the light of the garden of glory into the darkness of the outside world. Their spirit died that day when they believed a lie and broke Elohim's Commandment. Since then the world has known sin and Satan and has not had the knowledge of the glory.

Yeshua came to restore us to the presence of the Almighty. He paid the price with His precious blood to buy us back from the devil! When we repent from our sinful ways and make Him the king of our lives, He comes in with His Holy Spirit and begins to restore us to His image and likeness, just like Adam was. That is why he is called the last

Adam! However, if we go ahead and keep breaking God's Commandments, we will still suffer the same consequences that Adam suffered. We die spiritually and we are cast out into the darkness! Yahveh has been merciful towards the ignorance of His people, but now He wants us to repent and let the Torah, His laws, the knowledge of the glory of God to be written in all our hearts. Then He wants us to *go* and fulfill the great commission of setting nations *free* through the power of the gospel, through His authority and teaching them to obey His Commandments!

The same serpent came back to tempt the woman, this time the church, the wife of the lamb, 1,600 years ago and said to her, "Surely it is okay to break God's Commandments and compromise the gospel in order to have peace and safety and to stop the persecution. Surely Constantine will be a good king and he will take care of you if you remove these Jews and this "Old Testament" from you! Just come and celebrate our pagan holidays, we will 'Christianize them' for you. Come and eat all the pork you want, and don't worry about the consequences! After all Jesus Christ came to extend grace so you could sin without guilt. Go ahead and break God's Commandments, those despicable Jewish laws and be free from their tyranny! *Come be free like all of us in the Roman Empire!*

Just like Adam and his wife were thrown out of the glorious presence of the Creator, so did the church of that time lose the presence of the glory and the knowledge of the glory of Yahveh. She was cast into the dark ages and began to sin more and more until she became a murderer and killed the mother that gave her birth—the Jews, the people of Israel.

"For the wages of sin is death and the gift of God is eternal life through Yeshua the Messiah our Lord."

— Romans 6:23

Think about it, every time that you sin death comes into your life. That is why when Ananias and Saphiras lied they instantly died; but even if you do not die physically immediately, death comes in, both to your spirit, your soul (depression), your body (sickness), your finances (debts, lack) and your family (strife, divorce, problem children).

If you truly repent of your sin and forsake it, He is merciful and just, to forgive you and to cleanse you from all unrighteousness (1 John 1:9). However, the seeds of death that you sowed, the seeds of sin and rebellion are still in the ground and bearing fruit.

The only way to counteract the effects of sin is by repentance, forgiveness and obedience. You need to actively sow obedience into your life. Begin to sow to the Spirit and you will reap. Let your *obedience spiritual crop* be greater than your *disobedience crop*!

When you repent, you are instantly forgiven, but your circumstances only change as you faithfully, diligently, perseveringly and solidly walk in obedience.

Many people are bitter with God and very discouraged because after they turned around and forsook their sin, their circumstances were still hard. It is because of the previous bad sowing but take a wise word of advice—do not concentrate on the circumstances, just keep on sowing obedience and righteousness, and one day you will see that the good crop has overtaken the bad and your circumstances will change!

It is so serious to disobey the Father, it is so serious to break His Commandments, that even after you are forgiven, and the consequences of sin are there. That is why when King David sinned and repented, though he was forgiven, he still suffered the consequences of his sin. Absalom, his Son, rebelled against him and tried to take his place as king, and Amnon, his other Son, raped his daughter, Tamar. Yet, God called David, *"A man after my own heart"* because David humbled himself, repented and never did it again.

The Word says that whatever a man sows he will reap. That includes our bad sowing. So after repentance and forgiveness we must concentrate on obedience and *good sowing.* Don't even bother with trying to resolve your ugly circumstances, just keep on obeying Yahveh and sowing right and in *due season,* your *good crop* will overtake the bad one!

The spirit of Constantine and replacement theology has filled the earth with the knowledge of Babylonian and pagan feasts, and with hatred towards the Torah and the Jewish people.

That has been a horrible sowing that is affecting all the nations right now!

So the Spirit of truth, the preaching of the true gospel and the teaching of Yah's Commandments will fill the earth with the knowledge of the glory of YHVH just like the waters cover the sea! We need to run now with the truth because the world is on the verge of a collapse.

We need to sow right, sow fast and sow a lot of good seeds! You and I have been appointed by the Almighty to change the world with truth and light and with the knowledge of the glory. Will you follow?

"Do not be deceived. God is not mocked; for whatever a man sows that will he also reap. For the one who sows to his own flesh (disobeys and breaks Yah's Commandments) will from the flesh reap corruption, but the one who sows to the Spirit will from the Spirit reap eternal life. Let us not lose heart in doing good, for in due time we will reap if we do not grow weary."

— Galatians 6:7-9

In order for you to be a leader, you need to learn to follow and become a disciple. So, let me fulfill the great commission with you and teach you God's Commandments, let me teach you Torah. As you open your heart to the Holy Spirit, to the anointing that dwells within you, He will teach you as you read, and He will write it into your heart. You will be able to understand the Word like never before and all confusion will leave you!

"The fear of Yahveh is the beginning of wisdom; a good understanding has all those who do His Commandments. His praise endures forever."

— Psalms 111:10

A Prayer of Repentance

Dear heavenly Father, I realize that I have believed a false gospel and I have taken Your Commandments and personal instructions to me very lightly. I have justified sin in my life and have not had a true knowledge of Your glory! Please forgive me for being lukewarm. I repent, turn around and am willing to 'buy gold refined in the fire, white garments and eye salve.' Whatever it costs I am willing to go with You all the way and to obey You all the way. Please forgive me for taking You and Your Word lightly. Please use me from now on to fill the world with the knowledge of Your glory. Help me to sow an abundance of good and holy seeds into this world. I am Yours forever and without reservations! In Yeshua's name. Amen.

.

CHAPTER EIGHT:

Torah Made Simple

"Behold days are coming, declares Yahveh, when I will make a new covenant with the house of Israel and with the house of Judah... But this is the covenant that I will make with the house of Israel after those days", declares Yahveh, "I will put My law within them and on their heart, I will write it; and I will be their Elohim and they will be My people."

— Jeremiah 31:31, 33

F irst of all, I want to call your attention to the fact that there is no new covenant without Judah and Israel. The new covenant is promised to them only! And through Israel, the Gentiles come in! Now, new covenant in Hebrew is *Brit Chadasha*, which could also be translated as a "Renewed Covenant." You see, the only ones that had a covenant with YHVH were the Jewish people, the children of Israel. Therefore, the Father has kept His promise given to Israel by sending His Son, the Messiah.

The only mark of the New Covenant is this: *"I will put My law within them and on their heart, I will write it"*

So, a true new covenant believer should have the law of God written in his heart! Where can you find that law? Of course, in the Hebrew Holy Scriptures, which we already know has been incorrectly called the "Old Testament." And how does Yahveh write in the heart of a believer? By the indelible pen of the Holy Spirit, who is the finger of God. Let us look at the function of the Holy Spirit who is God's presence in us, He is Yahveh Himself!

"But when the Spirit of truth comes, He will guide you into all truth; for He will not speak on His own initiative, but whatever He hears, He will speak; and He will disclose to you what is to come."

— John 16:13

Another word for describing the Holy Spirit is as the Anointing:

"As for you, the anointing which you received from Him abides in you, and you have no need for anyone to teach you; but as His anointing teaches you about all things, and is true and is not a lie and just as it has taught you, you abide in Him."

— 1 John 2:27

So, we can see that the Holy Spirit and the anointing *inside* of us:

- Guides us into all truth
- Teaches us all things

It will be the Holy Spirit within us that will write the Word of God, the Torah laws, in our heart. As we read it and meditate upon it, He will be doing His work.

A Prayer to Receive the Spirit of Truth and the Anointing

Dear heavenly Father, thank You for sending Yeshua, the Jewish Messiah, Your Son, to pay the price for my sins with His bloodshed for me at the cross. I believe that Yeshua is Yahveh, God and that He rose from the dead on the third day. I receive you Yeshua as my Savior and Master. I am willing to walk in obedience to you and to Your Word. I repent from all known and unknown sin in my life; I reject Satan and all his works. I break any unholy vows or covenants that I have made with other Gods. I thank you for receiving me into Your family and for washing me clean from all unrighteousness. I will cleanse my home from all unholy objects. Now I ask you to fill me with Your Holy Spirit, the Spirit of truth and to give me the anointing that teaches me all things. I stand by faith that I receive it in Yeshua's name. Amen.

Now, raise your hands to the Father and worship Him. You might feel an immediate difference and even begin to pray in a strange language. This is a prayer language that the Holy Spirit gives and it is wonderful. All believers in the early church had it when they received the baptism of the Holy Spirit and fire! (See Acts 2)

Laws, Statutes & Precepts

Once you understand how to relate to the Word, it will be very easy for you to hear the Holy Spirit and receive clear guidance from Him. Now, as you open the Word from the book of Genesis, you will allow the Holy Spirit to teach you, guide you and reveal Yah's will for you! It is interesting that already in the book of Genesis we can see that obedience to God's laws brings in the blessing. When Elohim appeared to Isaac in Gerar, He promised to bless Isaac,

"Because Abraham obeyed Me and kept My charge, My Commandments, My statutes and My laws."

— Genesis 26:5

The blessing to Abraham's Son, Isaac, was connected with the obedience of his father. Dear parents, even today as you choose to walk in obedience to Yah, you are building up a godly inheritance of blessing for your children. It is never too late to begin establishing a new inheritance of blessing in your family! This includes obedience not only to the written Commandments but to those that He gives you personally; it is obedience to all that He calls you to do! (See Deuteronomy 28:1-14)

Now, how did Abraham know about Torah, about Yah's laws? The Five Books of Moses were not written yet, the giving of the tablets of the law in Mount Sinai had not happened yet, so how did he know? In the same way that Adam knew in the garden; Elohim Himself taught His laws to Abraham! In other words, the Law given at Mount Sinai is not an "Old Testament" law as most preachers have taught, but rather an *eternal law.* Abraham already knew it and he understood the difference between Commandments, statutes and laws (or precepts).

In the Book of Nehemiah, we can see again this order:

"So, you made known to them Your Holy Sabbath, and laid down for them Commandments, statutes and law."

— Nehemiah 9:14

The words in Hebrew are:
- *Mitzvot* – "Commandments"
- *Hukim* – "Statutes"
- *Torah* – "Laws or precepts"

When we talk about all of Yahveh's instructions in righteousness we call it by the name of Torah as a general term.

The Torah has been given to the people of Israel by YHVH in order to show and demonstrate His ways to the world. This was not only given for the Jewish people to keep these marvelous instructions for themselves but rather for us to share them with the entire world and thus bring the world into the ways of *the blessing.*

The whole notion about Torah is very different than most western ideas of '*Law.*' The western idea of law is very dry, ruthless and sometimes even illogical. However, Torah is mostly loving & caring, and it makes complete sense. It is very important that you understand this: Yah did not give us laws because He is sitting in heaven as a dictator and wants to 'play king' with us. His laws and Commandments, called *Torah*, are given to us for a few reasons:

1. To show us the way of holiness for He is holy
2. To teach us the ways of the Kingdom of Yah because after the *fall*, man lost those ways.
3. To instruct us on how to stay healthy and blessed in spirit, soul and body.

The purpose of His Torah was not to make life miserable for us, but rather to help us live this life on earth full of holiness, purity, blessing, fruitfulness and satisfaction. And when we choose His Torah instructions after we are born again, they still work for us today, just like they worked for Noah, Abraham, Moses, David and Yeshua!

The God of Israel is a God of plenty, of abundance, of greatness and He is a *lover*. He is *love* Himself and He hates to see the people that He created disconnected from the abundant life of His Kingdom. That is why He said so clearly in John 10:10: *"The thief did not come but to steal, kill and destroy. But I came to give your life and life more abundantly."*

Yeshua said that when we see Him, we see the Father[6]. The Word also says to walk just as Yeshua walked[7] and how did He walk? In obedience to His Father's Commandments,

---

6 John 14:9
7 1 John 2:6

and because of that, He was favored by His Father and could do so many miracles! The Word also tells us that *Yeshua learnt obedience by the things He suffered[8]*. He Himself had to learn and be instructed by the Torah to be obedient to His heavenly Father. That obedience caused Him to fulfill His calling as Messiah, raise the dead, heal the sick, open blind eyes and feed the thousands with almost no food!

In Deuteronomy 28:1-14 it is written so clearly that when we obey Yah's Commandments we will be the head and not the tail and that we will be blessed everywhere and in everything we do! The Holy Spirit has been given unto us in order to lead us to obedience and teach us the blessed ways of Yah that is the Torah.

The Holy Spirit interprets it to us: that is the new covenant according to Jeremiah 31:31-34, the marvelous blessing ways of Elohim which is the *Torah* written in our hearts. As we let it happen, we enter into another realm of the blessing and we wonder why did it take us so long to understand it and why did we oppose it for so long? My answer to that is that the devil lied to you in order to keep you lowly, sick, poor, weak, fruitless and small; but your Father in heaven loves you so much and if you listen to His instructions in the Torah, you will see it with your own eyes and feel it in your body, finances, family, job and everywhere.

Let us take a look at the Commandments, statutes and laws.

---

8   Hebrews 5:8

The Commandments – Mitzvot

These mostly relate to the Ten Commandments, that I have named "The Heavenly Constitution." These were given to Moses on Mount Sinai and they were written by the finger of God Himself! (See Exodus 20 and Deuteronomy 5)

"When He had finished speaking with him upon Mount Sinai, He gave Moses the two tablets of the testimony, tablets of stone written by the finger of God."

— Exodus 31:18

All the other laws given to Moses later on were written by the hand of Moses as he heard them from Yahveh but not the Ten Commandments; these were written by the finger of God! That shows us very clearly, that *no one* has the right to change them. These are eternal and immutable! When we break any of these, it causes death and curses to come into our lives – curses that are visited even up to the third and fourth generation.

"For I, Yahveh, am a jealous God, visiting the iniquity of the fathers on the children, on the third and fourth generation of those who hate me. But showing loving-kindness to thousands, to those who love Me and keep My Commandments."

— Exodus 20:5, 6

When we break any of His top ten, it causes a curse to come upon us and our children, and their children, etc. But when we obey them a blessing comes in even to a thousand generations! Look how good God is; if you just love Him and obey His Commandments, He gets beside Himself to bless you and 'splurge' the blessing on all of your descendants. Sometimes people that feel very blessed tell me: *"I must have done something good that things are going so well for me."* In most cases it is actually a father, a mother or a grandparent that obeyed Yah's Commandments. The children and grandchildren and even great grandchildren are enjoying the blessing. Someone sowed right!

The Ten Commandments

"I AM Yahveh your Elohim, who brought you out of the land of Egypt, out of the house of slavery.

You shall have no other Gods before me.

You shall not make for yourself an idol, or any likeness of what is in heaven above or on the earth beneath or in the water under the earth. You shall not worship them or serve them; for I, Yahveh your Elohim, am a jealous God visiting the iniquity of the fathers on the children, on the third and the fourth generations of those who hate me, but showing loving-kindness to thousands, to those who love me and keep my Commandments.

You shall not take the name of Yahveh your Elohim in vain, for Yahveh will not leave him unpunished who takes his name in vain.

Remember the Sabbath day, to keep it Holy. Six days you shall labor and do all your work, but the seventh day is a Sabbath of Yahveh your

Elohim; in it you shall not do any work, you or your Son or your daughter, or your male or your female servant, or your cattle, or your sojourner who stays with you. For in six days Yahveh made the heavens and the earth, the sea and all that is in them, and rested on the seventh day; therefore, Yahveh blessed the Sabbath day and made it Holy.

Honor your father and your mother that your days may be prolonged in the land which Yahveh your Elohim gives you.

You shall not murder.

You shall not commit adultery.

You shall not steal.

You shall not bear false witness against your neighbor.

You shall not covet your neighbor's house; you shall not covet your neighbor's wife or his male servant, or his female servant or his ox, or his donkey or anything that belongs to your neighbor."

— Exodus 20:3-17

The Commandments are eternal, unchangeable, and immutable and it is the foundation of life in the Kingdom of God. It is the constitution of heaven and the purpose of heaven is to bring this constitution down here to earth so that *all* nations may institute it and become *sheep nations!* (Matthew 25:32)

Yeshua expounded on some of these Commandments in Matthew 5:21-37 in such a serious way that He warned the people about breaking them or even thinking about breaking them. Even looking at a woman to lust after her incurs a serious judgment!

> "If your right eye makes you stumble, tear it out and throw it from you; for it is better for you to lose one of the parts of your body, than for your whole body to be thrown into hell. If your right hand makes you stumble, cut it off and throw it from you; for it is better for you to lose one of the parts of your body than for your whole body to go into hell."
>
> — Matthew 5:30, 31

Most of the pastors of today would not let Yeshua preach in their congregations, they would call Him legalistic and condemning! He is saying here that breaking Yahveh's Commandments can cause a person to go to hell. It is better to lose everything in life but not your salvation. Get rid of everything that causes you to sin, be hard on yourself, be tough on yourself, and deal with sin *ruthlessly!*

> "Our Father who is in heaven, hallowed be Your name. Your Kingdom come; Your will be done on earth as it is in heaven."
>
> — Matthew 6:9b-10

The Statutes – Hukim

The Statutes are the second group among Yah's laws. They are not written directly by the finger of God, but they were given directly by the Almighty to Moses (please remember that Abraham knew the statutes as well!)

The statutes are all the laws that instruct:

- How to worship the Almighty
- How to differentiate between the holy and the profane

Therefore, it includes all the laws that are connected with sacrifices, tithes, offerings, temple worship, social laws about orphans and widows, the dietary laws of clean and unclean animals, laws that forbid mixture, the laws of blood, and laws about morality. Because the statutes are connected with the separation between the holy and the profane and with holy worship, they will mostly be found in the Book of Leviticus.

The principle of the statutes is as eternal as the Commandments, but their specific application may change with the times. For example, today there is no temple in Jerusalem and there is no need for blood sacrifices for atonement as Yeshua is the ultimate blood sacrifice for sin's atonement. However, the body of the Messiah has become the temple of the Holy Spirit and the statutes give us much instruction on how to worship the Father in Spirit and truth. However, there are *perpetual* statutes that both the principle and the application are eternal,

"It is a perpetual statute throughout your generations in all your dwellings; you shall not eat any fat or any blood."

— Leviticus 3:17

A perpetual statute has almost the same level of importance as a Commandment.

So, are any statutes done away with? What about animal sacrifices?

These are fulfilled by the blood sacrifice of Yeshua; however, the principle is still for today through: repentance. When we ask for forgiveness and turn from sin, the Blood of the Lamb cleanses us and brings us into close communion with the Father.

The word sacrifice is *korban*, which comes from the word *Karob*, which means – *near or close*. The sacrifices in ancient times meant to bring the sinful people close to a holy God. When we repent, receive forgiveness and the cleansing of Yeshua's blood, communion with the Father is renewed!

"The sacrifices of Yahveh are a broken spirit; a broken and a contrite heart, O God, you will not despise."

— Psalm 51:17

Because so many of the statutes are connected with sacrifices and temple worship it is necessary to understand the statutes versus the finished work of Yeshua at the cross. While the principle of these laws is eternal, yet the applications of those laws are not. In that sense some statutes connected with temple worship and blood sacrifices have changed.

"If perfection was through the Levitical priesthood (for on the basis of it the people received the law), what further need was there for another priest to arise according to the order of Malchizedek and not be

designated according to the order of Aaron? For when the priesthood is changed, of necessity there takes place a change of law also."

— Hebrews 7:11, 12

This Scripture gives us an understanding on how to relate to all the laws of the priesthood and of temple worship. Their principles are eternal, but their applications have changed, since Yeshua has completed the payment in order to bring us back to Yahveh.

Important Statutes

Among the statutes, you will find out some that carry strong warnings such as, if you violate them, "you will be cut off from your people." Those deserve particular attention, as in most cases they are important for us today. Here is an example:

"If there is a man who lies with a menstruous woman and uncovers her nakedness, he has laid bare her flow, and she has exposed the flow of her blood, thus both of them shall be cut off from among their people."

— Leviticus 20:18

The Word instructs women to separate for seven days from the beginning of their period and not to have intercourse. (Leviticus 15:19). It is interesting to note that among Jewish women who keep this statute there is 0% of cervical cancer. Whereas among Christian women who do not honor this statute there is a high percentage of cervical cancer. I also believe that many of the feminine diseases, such as miscarriages, endometriosis and hysterectomies (removal of the uterus due to growths, cysts and the like) are related to the violation of this statute.

Among the statutes we will distinguish between creational statutes or laws and Moses law. Some of the statutes given to Moses are creational laws and as such they are unchangeable! Creational laws are those laws that are connected with the order of creation and many of them are already mentioned in the book of Genesis.

Creational Statutes

1. All the laws about the feasts that Yah calls my feasts. Those are mentioned in the Hebrew as *Moadim* or testimonials and they are already set at creation in Genesis 1:14 and explained in Leviticus 23 and in Numbers 28.

2. All the dietary laws connected with clean and unclean animals. Already in Genesis seven, we read that Noah brought into the Ark, two by two of the unclean or impure animals and seven by seven of the clean and the pure animals. All of Leviticus 11 is still for today. The animals have never changed! It is still not acceptable for a believer in the Holy God of Israel to consume those animals that He called unclean. (See chapter 9 for more explanations)

3. The statutes connected with consuming blood. This is a creational principle, in Leviticus 17:10-14 we learn that the 'life of the flesh is in the blood' and already in Genesis 9:4—*"Only you shall not eat flesh with its life, that is its*

blood."

4. The laws of first fruits is already implied in Genesis 4, when Cain brought an offering (any offering) to Elohim and Abel brought the *first* of his flock. The offering of Abel was accepted but that of Cain was not! The reason is that Cain did not bring a first fruit offering like he should have. Abel obeyed the statute and brought a first fruit offering.

5. The laws of tithing already appear in the Book of Genesis when Abraham gave Malchizedek, the king of Salem, (Genesis 14: 19, 20) a tithe of all that he had.

6. The laws about *no mixture*. Elohim created all plants, animals and humans according to their kind. That is why a crossing between a horse and a donkey breeds a mule, and a mule cannot reproduce. That is why God did not create transvestites and homosexuals. He created a man to be a man and a woman to be a woman. Every crossing of kinds is contrary to God's creational law and it causes confusion, pain and curses. *(See Genesis chapter one)*

"You are to keep My statutes." You shall not breed together two kinds of your cattle; you shall not sow your field with two kinds of seed, nor wear a garment upon you of two kinds of material (natural fibers) mixed together."

— Leviticus 19:19

7. The law of sowing and reaping confirmed to Noah after the flood, *"While the earth remains, seedtime and harvest and cold and heat, and summer and winter, and day*

and night shall not cease." Genesis 8:22

Important

Please note that I did not mention the Shabbat or other creational laws that are *Commandments*. As I have already shared previously, the ten Commandments are written by the finger of God and cannot be changed or tampered with. That is why it is so serious that for 1.600 years the church has been taught to break the Shabbat because of replacement theology. This has caused many curses, confusion, sickness, poverty and in general, lack of power and anointing. Since breaking any of the ten brings generational curses.

The Laws or Precepts – The Torah

The laws or the precepts are many in number and in fact, anyone who will walk with Yeshua will receive personal laws. The precepts have eternal value, but they are often temporary. They are the wisdom of God applied to a certain situation. Many people fall into 'legalism' when they take one of these precepts that were given to help in a particular situation and apply it to a non-related one. Let me give you an example,

In every house or congregation there are laws or precepts that will apply to that house, but they are not applicable in another house. In our congregation in Tel Aviv for example I had a precept or a law that when I began to preach, the door of the meeting room needed to be closed and people had to be quiet and not move around. While that has an eternal value that is connected with the fear of God and honoring the Word and the servant of Yah, yet the way each one applies this principle in their congregation may vary with the culture or with the upbringing. Maybe in other congregations it is okay to leave the door to the meeting hall opened! I certainly would be out of order if I would write a special letter to all congregations in the body, telling them that it is a sin to leave the door to the meeting hall open during the preaching of the message!

So, precepts or laws are very necessary, but they need to be revised once in a while and be open to change according to the times and the circumstances.

Let us see a very clear example of this in the Bible,

"You shall also have a place outside the camp and go out there, and you shall have a spade among your tools, and it shall be when you sit down outside, you shall dig with it and shall turn to cover up your excrement. Since Yahveh your Elohim walks in the midst of your camp to deliver you and to defeat your enemies before you, therefore your camp must be Holy; and He must not see anything indecent among you or He will turn away from you."

— Deuteronomy 23:12-14

The principle of this law is eternal. God is Holy; He wants us to keep cleanliness, hygiene, decency and purity within our living quarters. However, in those days there were no toilets and no indoor plumbing, so He gave them clear instructions as a father to children on how to keep their camp clean. Nowadays there are wonderful modern toilets, with great plumbing and drainage and I am positive that we are not sinning by having a toilet inside of our homes! We can take this precept and learn a lot about Yah's ways and how He expects us to keep our dwelling places in a manner that is pleasing unto Him. For example, is there anything indecent in your home from which He would turn away? Maybe you have some indecent pictures or magazines? Maybe the TV programs that you are watching or the music that you are listening to is indecent? Notice that He said that keeping clean and decent, holy and pure living quarters is connected with victory over your enemies! Maybe you need to do some house cleaning and burn some unholy items. Do not delay lest you are defeated before your enemies!

As you meditate on these laws and other laws and you seek Yahveh for their application, see what the Holy Spirit tells you and allow Him to write His laws and precepts in your heart and mind.

"This book of the law shall not depart from your mouth, but you shall meditate on it day and night, so that you may be careful to do according to all that is written in it; for then you will make your way prosperous, and then you will have success."

— Joshua 1:8

CHAPTER NINE:

Practical Life Applications – Part 1

"For just as the body without the spirit is dead, so faith without works is dead."

— Yaakov (James) 3:26

In the next two chapters, I will help you to put the Commandments and the creational statutes into practice. It is time to change your lifestyle! Now that you have believed in the truth of the gospel, it is time to put your faith into practice and put it to work.

Remember that Yeshua paid the price for all of your sins, so to the measure that you repent of them and put your trust in Him, you will be able to walk in newness of life. As you read every Commandment and its applications, allow the Holy Spirit to give you conviction of sin and deal with your heart. Then fall on your knees, confess them before the Father, accept forgiveness because of Yeshua's sacrifice and forsake sin. Live in His glory and presence! Let your life begin to shine!

Practical Applications of the Ten Commandments

First Commandment

You shall have no other Gods before Me.

— Exodus 20:11

This means that you cannot add Yahveh-Yeshua to your list of other Gods or beliefs. He is number one and the only one. That includes the God of money or mammon, the God of the new age, yoga and meditation, karate, kung-fu, Chinese medicine, Islam, Bahai, Buddhism, or any other religious practices. Even your job or your family can be a God to you. You need to check your heart that Yahveh-Yeshua reins sovereignly as the only God of your life.

Practical Applications

- Begin and end your day early in prayer and meditation in His Word.
- Think and talk to Him during the day constantly, think and speak His Word.
- Meet regularly with other believers in Messiah.
- Separate tithes and first fruit offerings and give them to those ministers who teach you the Word, minister

to you and that are doing God's work in Israel and the nations.

- Obey promptly all that He tells you to do with no excuses.
- Fast and pray often.
- Seek His face diligently.
- Share the good news of the gospel with others.
- Choose your friends from among those that are 'sold out' to Yeshua.
- Keep your heart, mind and mouth clean.
- Do not watch TV, Internet, read books, magazines or listen to music unless it is godly and gives Him glory. The rule of thumb is that if God would not watch it, you should not either.
- Computer games and Nintendo can be very harmful. Most of them are filled with violence and witchcraft. Remember that whatever you spend your time with, will become your friend and Your God.
- Cleanse your house or your room from all unholy, immoral, idolatrous and witchcraft objects. Destroy them and throw them out (Don't give them to someone else!).
- Be thankful and worshipful to Him at all times.
- Do what Yeshua would do at all times!

Second Commandment

You shall not make for yourself an idol, or any likeness of what is in heaven above or on the earth beneath or in the water under the earth. You shall not worship them or serve them; for I, Yahveh your Elohim, am a jealous God visiting the iniquity of the fathers on the children, on the third and the fourth generations of those who hate me, but showing loving-kindness to thousands, to those who love Me and keep My command.

— Exodus 20:12

Practical Applications

- All religious icons are idols. You should destroy those! (Virgin Mary, Saints, African masks, figurines of ancient Gods, Egyptian Papyruses etc...)
- Not all art is holy. Some sculptures and paintings are idolatrous, so be careful with what you decorate your home with!
- A person can be an idol to you. For example, pictures of immoral relationships of the past should be destroyed and thrown out, including valuable objects that are connected with that relationship. (Old wedding or engagement rings from other marriages, clothing that belonged to him/her, etc.)
- Any object that has an emotional/spiritual effect on you, to the point that you would never give it up, could be an idol. Pray about each one of those.

- All objects of superstition such as, the eye, the hand (Hamsa), the red thread, the pentagram (satanic star), and the hippie sign (broken cross or peace sign). Sometimes certain family memorabilia become a superstitious object of 'good luck.' (Not all symbols are superstitious objects, however if you trust in them to protect you or to defend you or to bring you 'good luck' that is an idol! However, some symbols are demonic identification signs and they bring in curses even if you don't trust in them!)
- Get rid of all witchcraft and new age objects! Be serious and thorough!

Third Commandment

You shall not take the name of Yahveh your Elohim in vain, for Yahveh will not leave him unpunished who takes His name in vain.

— Exodus 20:13

Practical Applications

- Be careful with colloquial expressions such as for "For God's sake" or "God knows" or any other manners of speech that use His name lightly. Change your vocabulary.
- Do not say 'God told me' or "God/Yahveh showed me' unless you are sure about it. If you are sure by all means say it.

- Be careful with your tongue, try to use expressions such as, "I believe that God told me", "I feel that Yahveh showed me."
- Be free in using His holy name as long as it is with love, respect, reverence and the holy, healthy fear of God.
- Do not use His name to manipulate people to do your will!
- Think twice before you speak about Him.
- Pray every day this prayer: *Yahveh, glorify Your name in me.*

Fourth Commandment

Remember the Sabbath day, to keep it Holy. Six days you shall labor and do all your work, but the seventh day is a Sabbath of Yahveh your Elohim; in it you shall not do any work, you or your Son or your daughter, or your male or your female servant, or your cattle, or your sojourner who stays with you. For in six days Yahveh made the heavens and the earth, the sea and all that is in them, and rested on the seventh day; therefore, Yahveh blessed the Sabbath day and made it Holy.

— Exodus 20:14

In order to keep the Shabbat holy, we need to take into consideration what the Fourth Commandment says, what the creational law says and also what are the statutes given for the Shabbat.

Yahveh also gave some precepts, that though the principle is eternal, yet the application will vary according to the times and the culture. Shabbat can become cumbersome when some laws that applied to the life of Israel in the desert are applied to our modern-day lifestyle. For example:

"You shall not kindle a fire in any of your dwellings on the Sabbath day."

— Exodus 35:3

Later on, we see that a man was defiling the Shabbat by gathering wood on the Shabbat in order to kindle a fire. Yah ordered to stone him to death. (Numbers 16:32-35). The reason for that is stated in the previous verse to this event: *"But the person that does anything defiantly, whether he is native or an alien, that one is blaspheming Yahveh; and that person shall be cut off from among his people. Because he has despised the Word of Yahveh and has broken His Commandments, that person shall be completely cut off; his guilt will be on him."* Exodus 34:30-31. The *key* issue here was defiance, he was sinning intentionally, and intentional sin incurs immediate punishment in any legal system!

But what about the 'kindling of fire'? Is this allowed in the Sabbath day? This is my opinion about this issue: The way I see it is that at that time, the kindling of fire was a very complicated job that took many hours. Nowadays one can strike a match or put on a light switch! It does not steal any time from the Shabbat, and it can actually help us to study His Word all the way into the night. In this case technology is put at the service of the Shabbat. This precept, (in my opinion) applied to Israel in the desert but it does not apply to us in modern day cities.

The eternal principle is: Do not detract from the Shabbat day by doing other jobs that eat up your time, and do not break Yah's laws intentionally and defiantly!

"The fear of Yahveh is the beginning of wisdom. A good understanding has all those who keep His Commandments."

— Psalm 111:10

Practical Applications to the Commandment of the Sabbath

- Separate the day from Friday sunset to Saturday sunset.

- Mark it and make it special by the following suggestions (suggestions are NOT Commandments!): 1. A special, very festive family dinner with a white table cloth. 2. Taking the bread and the wine as in Communion, 3. Share from the Torah portion that is read in all the synagogues. 4. Husbands, bless your wife by declaring Proverbs 31: 10-31. Wives, bless your husband and declare over them Psalms One. Both husband and wife, bless your children by declaring the Aaronic prayer found in the Book of Numbers, chapter 6:22-27. 5. Worship and sing to Yah around the dinner table. (The Jewish people also mark it by the lighting of two candles before sunset.

The wife, the husband and the children take special baths and even ritual baths called Mikveh before the Shabbat to prepare themselves as for a wedding!). You can pray and the Holy Spirit will give you creative ideas on how to sanctify it or set it apart as special. The key is to honor Yahveh and honor the Commandment.

- Do not work on Shabbat in order to earn money. Give this day to Yahveh in order to worship Him, study the Word and meet with other believers. (You will have to seek Him about what to do if you have a job that requires work on the Sabbath. He knows your struggles and if you put Him first and seek Him on how to make the change, He will guide you. It will require faith from your part to obey Him. However, He will provide for you and you will be the head and not the tail. Just follow the Holy Spirit's instruction on how to make the change.)

- Refrain from doing your regular housework, washing, shopping, car cleaning, etc. on this day. Do these on any other day! Do your cooking before Shabbat, so that you only warm up the food or eat it cold. The key is to get *unbusy* from the things you have to always do, so you have time to spend in the Word and in prayer, with your family and with other believers. (In our family, especially since we have a traveling ministry, we do eat the festive Shabbat dinner in restaurants.)

- Shabbat is not a good day to go to water parks, amusement parks and the like as it is a day to seek Yah, to pray, worship and to study the Word. It has to be different than all your other days! You recharge your spiritual batteries on that day!

- The only ones that worked on Shabbat were the priests that officiated at the temple. They rested when their shift was over. In the same way, those that are in active ministry, should be teaching and serving the people on Shabbat and take their physical rest another day.

- Traveling on Shabbat should be limited to those necessary trips in order to meet with other believers to worship, or if you are a minister and you need to travel or fly to your meeting. However, I believe that the best is to arrive a day earlier and stay close to the meeting place as traveling and flying take too much energy and time.

- Do not do sales on Shabbat. You can close your shop on Friday before sun set and reopen on Saturday night. We do that even with our resource book table during our ministry conferences and Yah blesses us for it!

- There are important statutes about offerings and sacrifices on Shabbat, so Shabbat is definitely a day to give and receive offerings.

- Whatever steals your time from studying the Word, prayer, worship and fellowship in the spirit should be kept out of your Shabbat. That includes TV, unless it is a godly program that the Holy Spirit is leading you to watch. Remember that the rest of the week will be hectic, and this is the only day to be refreshed physically and spiritually, and it is the only day that your family can spend together in God.

- Shabbat is an anointed, blessed and holy day. As such, it is the most wonderful way to minister healing and bless people with Yahveh's goodness!

- Delight yourself in the Shabbat! In other words, do not become religious but exercise the principle that this is a day to spend in His presence and in the presence of His people and *"In Your Presence is fullness of joy; in Your right hand there are pleasures forever."* Psalm 16:11

Other Scriptures about the Shabbat: Genesis 2:1-3, Deuteronomy 5: 12-15, Nehemiah 10:31, 1 Chronicles 23:31, Leviticus 23:38, Numbers 28:9, Isaiah 56, Mark 3:4, Luke 6:9.

Fifth Commandment

Honor your father and your mother that your days may be prolonged in the land which Yahveh Elohim gives you.

— Exodus 20:15

This is one of the most violated Commandments in this modern-day society, and the fruit of it is clearly seen in the children and in the youth. Teen pregnancies and teen suicides have been on the increase all the time. So many young people are drug addicts and criminals. The psychiatric wards are full! Since breaking any of Yah's Ten Commandments brings generational curses, we can see clear patterns of depression, suicide and addiction repeating themselves in three generations. The grandfather, the father and the Son! Since this is happening in the church in almost the same magnitude than outside, this is a direct outcome of rejecting and breaking Yah's Commandments because of replacement theology:

"My people are destroyed for lack of knowledge, because you have rejected knowledge, I also will reject you from being my priest (See Chapter 6, the knowledge of the glory!). Since you have forgotten the law of Your God, I will also forget your children."

— Hosea 4:6

"Remember the law of Moses My servant even the statutes and the ordinances which I commanded him in Horeb for all of Israel. Behold I am going to send you Elijah the prophet before the coming of the great and terrible day of Yahveh. He will restore the hearts of the fathers to the children and the hearts of the children to the fathers, so that I will not come and smite the land with a curse."

— Malachi 4:4-6

Since parents represent the authority of Yahveh on earth it is absolutely deathly to dishonor parents. When the church rebelled against the Jewish Roots and their Jewish parents, she broke this Commandment and death came in! The turning of Gentile believers and Christians back to the Jewish biblical roots and to honor Israel and the Jewish people is a matter of life and death!

It was to Abraham as the father of Israel that Elohim promised,

"I will bless those who bless you and curse those who take you lightly and dishonor you!"

— (Genesis 12:3 paraphrased from the Hebrew)

God gave Abraham and his descendants this promise because Israel is the spiritual mother of the nations, and through Yeshua the Jewish Messiah, some Jews became the Apostolic Fathers of the church!

Disrespecting and disregarding Israel is like breaking the fifth Commandment. This Commandment is so serious (they all are) that even when a father sins, children are still required to honor that father. In some cases, some criminal and sinful parents cannot be followed or obeyed but they need to be forgiven and honored! (See Genesis 9:20-29 when Noah was drunk, and his nakedness was uncovered.)

Practical Applications

- Repent for dishonoring your parents, in word, deed or attitude. Develop a habit of respect towards your parents, even in your tone of voice. Humble your heart.

- Repent for disrespecting or despising any pastor and leader, even if you are not able to follow them anymore. Forgive them for their sin, if they have sinned.
- Take the godly instructions of your parents and pastors very seriously.
- Be careful on how you joke with your parents, they are not your 'buddies', though if you are obedient, they will become your friends.
- Do not throw tantrums or try to manipulate your parents to make them do what you want.
- Be prompt to obey with all respect.
- Be an example to others on how to treat your parents, be different than the rest!
- Care for your parents when they are old and sick, to the best of your ability.
- Whatever you do as unto Yahveh, do it also to bring honor to your parents.
- Honoring your parents does not mean that you allow yourself to be abused or manipulated; it rather means that you maintain a humble attitude towards them even when they are wrong.
- Maybe you are an adult now and you have rebellious or disrespectful children. I suggest that you repent for the sins that you have committed against your parents and if at all possible, that you ask them for

forgiveness. As you do that and you also forgive your parents, then go ahead and pray,

"Dear Father in heaven, thank you for forgiving me for disrespecting my own parents. From now on I honor them and ask you to remove every curse that has fallen on me and my children for my disobedience." In Yeshua's name. Amen.

Sixth Commandment

You shall not murder.

— Exodus 20:16

Practical Applications

- Do not physically harm or kill someone.
- Do not kill someone with your tongue through slander, gossip and evil speech; do not ruin other people's reputations! (James 3)
- Do not kill someone in your heart by hating them. (Matthew 5:21-24)
- Forgive and release people. If you do not, God will not forgive you either. (Matthew 6:15)
- Be truthful without being hurtful. (Ephesians 4:15)
- Cleanse your mind and heart from thoughts of vengeance. (Romans 12:19)
- Repent for all jealousy. Cain murdered his brother because he was jealous. (Genesis 4, Song of Solomon

8:6) The devil was a murderer from the beginning. He came to steal, kill and destroy. (John 10:10 , read Matthew 5:21-24)

"Blessed are those who wash their robes, so that they may have the right to the tree of life and may enter by the gate into the city. Outside are the dogs, and the sorcerers, and the immoral persons *and the murderers* and the idolaters, and everyone who loves and practices lying."

— Revelation 22:14-15

Murderers can be saved, but they must repent and accept Yeshua's blood sacrifice at the cross. Paul was a religious murderer; he was killing the disciples in Messiah. He turned around to obedience to Messiah and became one of the greatest apostles that ever lived! If you were a murderer, invest you whole being in bringing life through the gospel!

Seventh Commandment

You shall not commit adultery.

— Exodus 20:17

This Commandment covers all the range of sexual immorality and fornication as in Hebrew it says *lo tinaf*, which includes fornication. Fornication is any kind of sex outside of holy marriage.

Practical Applications

- Decide that you will stay a virgin until your wedding and ask God for your right mate.
- Do not date the opposite sex in order to have fun. That leads always to immorality.
- If you date someone, it is because you are thinking about marriage. Keep your date in a public place and respect her/ him by not touching their bodies in a sexual manner.
- Repent and refrain from all pornography in magazines, films or the internet.
- Cleanse your heart and mind from sexual and immoral thoughts towards women or men.
- Do not share an apartment with single people of the opposite sex. Keep your life pure.
- Go to a good ministry of deliverance and ask them to pray for you, if you are experiencing dreams or lustful thoughts.
- Fill yourself with Yah's Word; meditate on it day and night. Fill your thoughts with His Word, worship and prayer.
- Change your TV programs to godly programs or quit TV altogether! Most of the programs, including the 'family programs' are filled with sexual immorality and filthy speech together with perverted values.
- Remember that even a kiss can cause two souls to be bound together that are not supposed to.

- Evil spirits move through sexual intercourse, so when you go to bed with someone that you are not married to, you can end with a venereal disease or *aids* and with unclean spirits.
- Fornication breaks your fellowship with the Holy Spirit and brings death to your life.
- Homosexuality and lesbianism is a gross immorality. It is totally perverted and in rebellion with Elohim the Creator. Homosexuals can be saved, and they need to repent and turn away from their sin just like everyone else! It is advisable to also receive deliverance from an anointed deliverance ministry. I suggest this site in the internet for more information: www. warfareplus.com
- Masturbation is a form of homosexuality or lesbianism with yourself and it is also a perversion. (See also Genesis 38:9-10 on 'spilling the seed').
- Watch the way you dress! God did not call us to be 'fashionable.' He called us to be holy even in the way we dress! Cover your feminine parts, your belly and be careful not to use seductive clothing. Let the way you dress show that you are a Son and a daughter of the Most High! Seductive clothing (short shirts that expose your belly or your breasts, short miniskirts, etc.) is meant to attract sexually. Do not be naïve and ungodly and do not give place to the devil! (1 Timothy 2:8-9)
- Cultivate a healthy fear of God in your life style.

- Change your friends! Choose friends that walk in holiness and in righteousness.

Yeshua was very radical in His teaching about sin and immorality. He said that we needed to deal ruthlessly with sin in our lives! Your hatred and rejection of sin is the *key* for your salvation. No one that loves sin can be saved; you can only be saved to the extent that you are sorry for breaking Yah's Commandments.

When you realize your need to live holy and to receive forgiveness then true repentance comes in. Repentance means that you *turn around* and go back to God, rejecting all that is filthy and ungodly in your life. You cannot love God and sin at the same time! So, go ahead *hate* sin with all of your heart and love Yeshua with all of your heart. *Be radical!*

"If your right eye makes you stumble, tear it out and throw it from you; for it is better for you to lose one of the parts of your body, than for your whole body to be thrown into hell. If your right hand makes you stumble, cut it off and throw it from you; *for it is better for you to lose one of the parts of your body than for your whole body to go into hell.*"

— Matthew 5:30, 31

"Or do you not know that the unrighteous will not inherit the Kingdom of God? *Do not be deceived;* neither fornicators, nor idolaters, nor adulterers, nor effeminates, nor homosexuals, nor thieves, nor the covetous, nor drunkards, nor revilers, nor swindlers will inherit the Kingdom of God. Such were some of you, but you were washed, you were sanctified, but you were justified in the name of Yeshua Messiah and in the Spirit of God."

— 1 Corinthians 6:9-11

"Blessed are those who wash their robes, so that they may have the right to the tree of life and may enter by the gate into the city. Outside are the dogs, and the sorcerers, and the immoral persons and the murderers and the idolaters, and everyone who loves and practices lying."

— Revelation 22:14, 15

Yeshua said that He will vomit out of His mouth anyone who is lukewarm, who compromises with sin and is not on fire for Yah and walks not in holiness and obedience. *Choose to become red hot!* Seek Him with all of your heart! (Revelation 3:14-22)

Repent and Choose Life!

Fall on your knees right now and pray and cry before God, repent be forgiven, be set free and change your lifestyle. You can!

Eighth Commandment

You shall not steal.

— Exodus 20:18

Practical Applications

- Do not take or 'borrow' without permission that which does not belong to you.
- Do not steal from God. Give your tithes, first fruit offerings and vows. (Malachi chapters 1-3, Deuteronomy 23:21)
- Be honest and straight in all your dealings!
- Keep your word in all areas of your life and especially when it is connected with finances.
- If you took something from someone, you need to pay him back from two to seven times more! That is called making restitution. (Exodus 22:4, 7, Proverbs 6:30, 31)
- Kidnapping is thieving, and it deserves death! (Deuteronomy 24:7)
- Theft brings shame and dishonor (Jeremiah 2:26). Stealing is deathly and it brings terrible curses to you and to your descendants. Thieves will not inherit the Kingdom of God. Thieving is a demonic spirit as satan is described as a thief that comes to steal, kill and destroy (John 10:10).

"Or do you not know that the unrighteous will not inherit the Kingdom of God? *Do not be deceived;* neither fornicators, nor idolaters, nor adulterers, nor effeminates, nor homosexuals, *nor thieves*, nor the covetous, nor drunkards, nor revilers, nor swindlers will inherit the Kingdom of God. Such were some of you, but you were washed, you were sanctified, but you were justified in the name of Yeshua Messiah and in the Spirit of God."

— 1 Corinthians 6:9-11

- Don't forget to deal ruthlessly with sin!

Ninth Commandment

You shall not bear false witness against your neighbor.

— Exodus 20:19

This Scripture in Hebrew means: You shall not lie about someone else or you shall not lie to someone else.

Practical Applications

- Lying begins in the heart. Watch and wash your heart!
- Adam and his wife fell because they believed a lie.
- Satan is the father of lies. So, liars make themselves to be Satan's children! (John 8:44)
- Lying to someone is to hate someone! (Proverbs 10:18, Proverbs 26:28)
- White lies are lies! (Proverbs 13:5)
- It is better to say nothing than to lie.
- Exaggerations are lies.
- Unbelief in God's Word and character is another form of believing a lie and lying to yourself in your heart. Get rid of all unbelief! This is how the snake

beguiled the woman; it accused Elohim's character and integrity.

- Fantasy and vain imaginations is playing with lies and it is deathly! (Genesis 6:5)
- Lying is a spirit that needs to be repented of and cast out! (1Kings 22)
- Many lies come in through watching TV. Quit watching all unholy programs and programs that do not build you up in God!
- Breaking your word and your promises is a form of lying. It leaves destroyed trust and relationships.
- Ask forgiveness from Yah and from all those to whom you have lied and see what you can do to restore trust. (1 John 1:9)
- Be consistent in keeping your word! (Psalm 15)

"There are six things which Yahveh hates, yes seven which are an abomination to Him. Haughty eyes, a lying tongue and hands that shed innocent blood. A heart that devises wicked plans, feet that run rapidly to evil. A false witness who utters lies and one who spreads strife among brothers."

— Proverbs 6:16, 17

King David said:

"I hate and abhor lying; but the law do I love."

— Psalm 119:163

Yeshua said:

"So Yeshua was saying to those Jews who had believed Him. "If you continue in My Word, then you are true disciples of Mine. And you will know the truth, and the truth will make you free."

— John 8:31-32

"But let your statement be YES, yes or NO, no; anything beyond these is evil."

— Matthew 5:37

Tenth Commandment

You shall not covet your neighbor's house; you shall not covet your neighbor's wife or his male servant, or his female servant or his ox, or his donkey or anything that belongs to your neighbor.

— Exodus 20:20

This sin is one of the sneakiest ones to detect, because it is in the heart. However, it can cause you to commit adultery, to lie, steal and even kill in order to obtain what you desire!

That is what happened to King David when he coveted Bathsheba. He ended up lying to Bathsheba's husband, Uriah the Hittite, and also scheming to kill him. He sent him to the hottest battle on purpose that he might lose his life! All that because he wanted to hide the fact that Bathsheba was pregnant because of his covetousness (2 Samuel 11)! So, because of covetousness David:

- Committed adultery and got Bathsheba pregnant.
- Lied to her husband Uriah.
- Killed her husband by putting him, on purpose, in the most dangerous place of the battle.

When Nathan the prophet confronted David with his sin, David humbled himself and repented before Yah. Even though God forgave him, the consequences of his sin followed him as he suffered some serious family difficulties later on!

Practical Applications

- Keep your heart and mind very clean. (Proverbs 4:23)
- Keep yourself busy doing the things of the Lord! Do not be idle.
- Watch out every time that you 'like' something or someone that belongs to someone else! Get your mind off them quickly!
- Be content for such things as you have! (Luke 3:14, 1 Timothy 6:8)
- Be thankful to Yah always, in everything and for everything. (Ephesians 5:20)
- Count your blessings. Meditate about all the things God has blessed you with.
- Make a covenant with your eyes and keep them fixed on Him!
- Be a hard and honest worker, persistent and diligent in your job. (Proverbs 10:4)

"Let your conversation be without covetousness; and be content with such things as ye have; for He has said, I will never leave thee nor forsake thee."

— Hebrews 13:5 KJV

"It is good to give thanks to Yahveh and to sing praises to Your name, O Most High; to declare Your loving-kindness in the morning and Your faithfulness by night."

— Psalms 92:1, 2

To sum this whole chapter up I say: Be humble of heart, have simple faith and trust in your Father in heaven, trust His Word and His promises, obey Him promptly, and do not delay! Thank Him always and in every situation, forgive every one that hurts you, betrays you and fails you and forgive yourself also. Love Yahveh with all of your heart, mind and strength; love the people that He created and sent His Son to die for and love yourself also!

Let the precious Holy Spirit lead you, guide you, comfort you, teach you and work mightily through you to bless, help and rescue many others.

"The conclusion, when all has been heard, is fear God and keep His Commandments, because this applies to every person. For God will bring every act to judgment, whether it is good or evil."

— Ecclesiastes 12:13, 14

CHAPTER TEN:
Walk in My Holy Feasts

"The one who says he abides in Him ought to, himself, walk in the same manner as He walked."

— I John 2:6

Yeshua walked in holiness and righteousness, honoring all the holy feasts and Moadim of His Father.

The three major testimonials, Moadim or holy convocations are pilgrim feasts and they are called *regalim*, from the word *regel*. Regel, means leg or foot in Hebrew. During those feasts one needed to 'walk towards the temple' in order to celebrate. There is a very close connection between the *regalim* and our walk with Messiah.

The holy feasts are, seven in number, and three of them are *regalim*.

- The Spring Feasts: Passover, Unleavened Bread, First Fruits, Shavuot (Pentecost)

- The Fall Feasts: Trumpets (Teruah, Rosh Hashanah), Atonement (Yom Hakippurim), Sukkoth (Booth, Tabernacles)

The order of these feasts is very revealing of the finished work of Messiah at the Cross. When we celebrate them, we can see the process that takes every believer in Yeshua from the act of *salvation* to the full work of *redemption*.

The biblical holy feasts that Yahveh calls My testimonials tell us the story of the full gospel from salvation to redemption. They teach us how to walk with God!

Salvation as Revealed in the Spring Feasts

Salvation in Hebrew is *Yeshuah*, which means "to rescue, to save, to deliver."

Pesach – Passover

Passover is celebrated between the 14th and the 15th of the biblical month Abib, the first month of the year. It is all about salvation by faith through grace. Its purpose is to remind us of the great salvation from death that Israel experienced in Egypt. As Yahveh instructed our people to put the blood of a perfect lamb on the lintels of the doors of their houses, the angel of death passed over the Israelites and killed the first born among the Egyptians. To celebrate, they had to eat the sacrificial Lamb roasted and they had to eat quickly, dressed up and ready to go out of Egypt and bondage! When salvation knocks on our door, we are to respond quickly, ready to follow Messiah, the sinless lamb. Through the blood of Messiah shed on the cross on a certain Passover around 2000 years ago, anyone that trusts and believes in Him can be saved from the slavery to sin and death. Many Gentiles took shelter in the house of the Israelites and joined them at that time for the Fear of Yahveh had fallen on them! (Exodus 12)

Feast of Unleavened Bread

Following the Passover meal, after the angel of destruction hit the Egyptians, they were to follow Moses into the wilderness. They had to leave Egypt *quickly*; so quickly that the bread dough did not have time to rise and it remained unleavened. So, they took this unleavened bread (called Matza today) into the desert with them and ate it there. We are to eat unleavened bread for seven days. In the same way once we accept the blood of Yeshua and salvation by faith through grace, we are to *flee* the bondage of *sin quickly*! So quickly that sin cannot catch up with us. Unleavened bread represents sinlessness. Yeshua is the Matza. He is the sinless, unleavened bread that came from heaven. When His blood washes us, He eradicates the body of sin out of our lives! And we have to do our part in fleeing from it *quickly*; quitting sin immediately after the *blood* has cleansed our hearts! This is repentance or turning from sin to Yah's right way of living.

First Fruits

The Feast of first fruits is celebrated the first day of the week, after the Shabbat that falls during the seven-day celebration of unleavened bread. Yeshua rose from the dead as Shabbat was finishing right as the feast of first fruits was entering in! He is the first fruits of those raised from the dead! That represents water baptism, right after salvation and repentance from sin. In water baptism by full immersion, we identify with Yeshua's death, burial and resurrection. We die with Him and rise into *newness of life*! Water baptism is the *first* Commandment given to those that repent of their sins and turn to the Messiah.

Shavuot – Pentecost

Shavuot (Pentecost) is the feast of bringing the first fruits of the grain harvest. This is also the time when the Torah was given on Mount Sinai. Approximately 2000 years ago, the Holy Spirit baptized the first Jewish church in Jerusalem, and they all spoke in tongues and began to win multitudes to the Messiah! As the Holy Spirit is poured out on us and fills us to overflowing, we will be empowered to preach the gospel with signs, wonders and miracles. It is the Holy Spirit that writes the Torah in our hearts so we will walk a holy walk!

So, the Fall Feasts take us from the salvation experience to repentance from sin, and to the beginning of a new life style filled with *Power!* Most of the church has stopped at *Passover*, which is salvation by faith through grace but has forgotten to *flee sin* and to rise in newness of life. That is why not many are *fully* baptized in the Holy Spirit with signs, wonders and miracles following. I invite you to celebrate all the feasts and come to the *fullness* of *salvation!*

A Life Changing Prayer

Dear heavenly Father, thank You for the revelation of Your Holy Feasts! Please forgive me for ignoring them. I accept the Passover Blood of the Lamb, Yeshua the Jewish Messiah and I *flee* immediately out of the bondage of sin and death! I reject and cast out of my life *all* that is evil in Your eyes! I proceed to the water of baptism by *full immersion*. I wait upon You ready and in obedience to fully baptize me in the Holy Spirit and fire. I receive Your full forgiveness now. In Yeshua's name. Amen.

Go ahead and make a change of life style, get rid of everything that displeases Yah! Get baptized in water by full immersion in the name of Yeshua. Go ahead and believe the Father to baptize you in the Holy Spirit. (Read Acts 2)

Let us now continue on to redemption!

Redemption as Revealed in the Fall Feasts

Redemption in Hebrew is *geula*, which means "to purchase in order to release," "set free," and "restore." (See Boaz the kinsman redeemer in the Book of Ruth, who purchased Naomi and all her inheritance in order to set them free from poverty and shame and restore them in *full* to Naomi's lost position as an honorable estate owner!) The work of *redemption* is what brings you and me and the entire Ecclesia to the greatness of Messiah and to His glory! There is no need to 'go to heaven' as the thief on the cross. We are called to be heirs and *co-heirs* with Messiah in order to rule and reign with Him! When the people of Israel left Egypt, they were all saved and rescued from Egypt. But only *two* from that generation made it to the promised land, their inheritance. Those were Joshua and Caleb who led the young generation in. Today there is a Joshua and Caleb company that is going to lead a young generation filled with faith and with the law of Yah written in their hearts into the *glory* of God.

Yom Teruah – The Feast of Trumpets

During this day of solemn convocation the Shofar horns are blown in order to call the people to full repentance from all their evil, sinful and compromised ways. This is a day that calls for judgment over sin and death. This day is followed by the Ten Days of Awe, also called "Hayamin Hanoraim" or the Terrible Days. These are days of serious soul searching, repentance and imploring Yah for mercy.

Yom Kippur – The Day of Atonement

This is the most holy day of the biblical calendar. The high priest presents two goats before Yah. One is called a *scapegoat* and the other one is the *sin atonement*. Yeshua was both the scapegoat and the sin atonement. The high priest confesses the sins of Israel as he lays hands on the scapegoat and then sends the scapegoat far away into the desert. "As far as the east is from the west, so far has He removed our transgressions from us." Psalm 103:12 The day of atonement is different than Passover as it pertains to forgiveness that comes from fully changing your ways into holiness! That is why Yom Hakippurim comes after the blowing of the shofars for repentance and is preceded by the "Ten Days of Awe" where everyone judges his/ her heart and life to see if they are pleasing to the Most High! A *bride*, pure and holy, without spot or wrinkle, is the result of this feast. At the end of the day of atonement, the last trumpet or last shofar is blown. Also, on the 50th year, which is the Year of Jubilee, in the day of atonement, the shofar of Jubilee is blown declaring *freedom* and restoration. (Leviticus 25:8-10). Yeshua paid the price not only to save us or rescue us from death but *to free* us *and restore us completely* to Yah's original plan for man to restore us to the perfection that existed before the fall of Adam. That is *redemption!* This feast is the feast of forgiveness to all those who have repented of their wicked ways and have been washed in the blood of the lamb. Yom Hakippurim is the mercy of God over His repentant people!

Sukkoth – The Feast of tabernacles

This feast marks the real time of birth of Messiah and is also a prophetic representation of the marriage supper of the lamb! It is the most joyous of feasts and all nations are commanded to celebrate it in the millennium (Zechariah 14:16) lest a curse would befall them! It is also the feast of ingathering of the *last harvest* and it is portrayed in Revelation 22:17— *"The spirit and the bride say, "Come, and let the one who hears say "come. And let the one who is thirsty come, let the one who wishes take the water of life without cost. "*

It will be a pure and holy bride restored to the position of royalty as Queen of Messiah, a royal priesthood and a holy nation that will be filled with His glory! It will be this glorious Ecclesia that will bring in the *last harvest of the nations*. This bride will be *completely free* from replacement theology and will be completely *grafted into* the olive tree of Israel. She will be like Ruth to the Jews and like Queen Esther on behalf of Israel! She will walk in the glory followed by astounding signs, wonders and miracles. She will preach an uncompromised gospel of repentance and multitudes will turn from unrighteousness to holiness in a short time! This awesome bride will present her king with many nations as *sheep nations*. Her mark will be the Torah written in her heart and mind, and she will walk in burning love and holiness. Her very presence will cause principalities to shake and Babylon to fall! The marks of the Fall Feasts are repentance, freedom and restoration.

"Arise and shine; for your light has come, and the glory of Yahveh has risen upon you. For behold darkness will cover the earth, and deep darkness the peoples; but Yahveh will rise upon you. Nations will come to your light, and kings to the brightness of your rising."

— Isaiah 60:1-3

This Scripture pertains to both the bride of Messiah and to Israel when she turns back to Yeshua as a nation.

Yeshua is inviting His entire body to come into the fall feasts. To turn from, compromise, tepidness, pride and ungodliness and to become pure and holy! The shofars are already blowing to call the bride to come home, to the original Apostolic, Jewish Foundations of the Faith!

The New Moon

"And it shall be that from New Moon to New Moon and from Sabbath to Sabbath, all mankind will come to bow down before me declares Yahveh."

— Isaiah 66:23

The New Moon or Rosh Chodesh celebrations are to be treated as a first fruits Shabbat unto Yah. Please note that *all* mankind will forever worship Him at that time, and this was set in motion already in Genesis 1:14! The laws of the new moon are the same in the Scriptures as those of the Shabbat and the Moadim—holy convocations. It is the first day of the month and like all *first* things they belong to Him. It is a perfect night for a night watch in your family and congregations! It is a time of renewal and of recommitment. You can mark it with a festive dinner (like Shabbat) and with a following prayer watch with other believers. The rest of the day you can spend studying His Word, worshipping and resting. If you have to work on that day and you are new at the feasts, please seek the Holy Spirit to give you wisdom. You can begin by separating it through a festive dinner and a following joint prayer meeting and or a night watch. It is commanded to blow the Shofar both before (full moon) and during this celebration (New Moon) like at the feast of trumpets. This is a call to return to Yah and to His ways. It is an important time of repentance, prayer, worship and transformation!

(See Numbers 10:10, Numbers 28:11, 1 Chronicles 23:31, 2 Chronicles 2:4, 2 Chronicles 8:15, Nehemiah 8:33, psalm 81:3, Ezekiel 46:2-4).

"Blow the trumpet at the new moon, at the full moon, on our feast day. For it is a statute in Israel, an ordinance of the God of Jacob. He established it as a testimony in Joseph."

— Psalm 81:3, 4

CHAPTER ELEVEN:
Practical Life Applications – Part Two

"The one who says he abides in Him ought himself to walk in the same manner as He walked."

— 1 John 2:6

This chapter is a practical chapter to help you celebrate His feasts. The purpose of this chapter is to make it easy for you. Do not be religious or rigid; let the Holy Spirit guide you through!

I will give your ideas on how to celebrate the different feasts; however, you can seek the Father on what would work well in your family and culture. I always make a distinction between law and tradition. Traditions are very important, but they don't carry the same weight!

Creational Statutes Applications — My Feasts

- I suggest that you get a Hebrew Messianic calendar with all the Torah readings for every Shabbat and every feast and with the dates for the feasts. The Hebrew biblical calendar is different than the Gregorian one as it is ruled by the sun and the moon. Remember that a biblical day begins and ends at sunset.

- Remember that every one of His feasts, His Moadim is a testimonial when He testifies about Himself, so each one of the celebrations is a testimony to His greatness and goodness!

- Purchase a Messianic Haggadah, the order of the ceremony of Passover, which can be found in most Christian book stores today. This little book is very good and helpful. You can choose to celebrate each feast by separating that specific time with Yah in order to seek Him and worship Him in communion with other believers. Even if you do not have the Haggadah, you can still show up for that date and meet with God!

- During the feasts, it is right to bring special festive offerings of the best that you have to Yahveh. The Word admonishes us not to come before the presence of the Lord with empty hands. (Exodus 23:15, Exodus 34:20, Deuteronomy 16:16) During the feasts there were always more sacrifices at the Temple.

- There is plenty of grace for you to learn about the feasts and how to celebrate them.
- It is always a good idea to be connected with a Messianic Jewish ministry to help you along.

Creational Statute # 1 – The Moadim Feasts

"Then Elohim said, 'let there be lights in the expanse of the heavens to separate the day from the night and let them be for signs and for seasons (Moadim) and for days and for years."

— Genesis 1:14

"Yahveh spoke again to Moses, saying, "Speak to the Sons of Israel and say to them, Yahveh's appointed times (Moadim) which you shall proclaim as Holy convocations-My appointed times (Moadim) are these: For six days work may be done, but on the seventh day there is a Sabbath to Yahveh in all your dwellings. These are the appointed times (Moadim) of Yahveh, which you shall proclaim at the times appointed for them."

— Leviticus 23:1-4

The Spring Feasts Fulfilled by Yeshua

Passover & Unleavened Bread

This is one of the *Regalim* or pilgrimage feasts where all the men of Israel were required to do a pilgrimage to Jerusalem, to the holy temple together with their families and worship Yahveh there for seven days. The first and the last days are a Shabbat where no regular work is done. (Read Leviticus 23:5-8)

On the first day and on the last day is a holy convocation that is treated just like Shabbat. In between is the Feast of unleavened bread, where we eat only Matzá or any unleavened bread, (bread with no leavening agents) to remember the fact that when our people left Egypt the bread had no time to rise, so they ate it flat. It has a deeper meaning that is very much connected with salvation. When you accept Yeshua as your Savior and Master, you have to flee the Egypt of sin so fast that there is no time for compromise to rise in your heart. In other words, repent from sin, accept forgiveness (His blood!), get cleansed from sin and do not let it rise in your heart again. Be quick to come out of Egypt! The Matzá bread is pierced, (has holes) and is striped and it represents Yeshua's wounded body for us at the cross (Isaiah 53). Leaven always represents sin, so unleavened bread is like Messiah who had no sin and was our lamb that gave His life for us that we might be rescued. One day before Passover make sure that you cleanse your house from all leaven, bread and leavening agents and most important that you cleanse your heart and life from all sin. On the last day, holy convocation can be marked by a festive meal again and a thanksgiving service around the table, where everyone shares his own experience of salvation and deliverance and what Yah has revealed during this Passover.

- The purpose of this feast is to remember the blood of the perfect lamb on the door posts that rescued Israel from the plague of the first born, the exodus from Egypt and deliverance from slavery.
- Yeshua was crucified at Passover at the same time that the Passover lambs were being slaughtered at the temple in Jerusalem.
- Yeshua's blood sacrifice delivered us from slavery to sin.
- The first day is a holy convocation or a Shabbat and it is treated like a Shabbat, except that we eat no leaven and no leavened bread. (See instructions for Shabbat)
- The Last Supper of Yeshua was a Passover meal.
- Make a very festive dinner and use Matzá or unleavened bread instead of bread.
- The father of the family, together with the mother, preside over the Passover meal.
- The Passover meal is like a "church service" around the table.
- Have everyone participate by giving them portions to read, prayers to lead, a song to sing or a drama to act. This should be a very exciting and fun time.

- Before the Passover meal it is a good time to read the story of the Exodus from the Scriptures and also the story of the Last Supper and of the death, burial and resurrection of Yeshua. (Exodus chapter 1 to Chapter 12 or at least all of chapter 12, Luke 22 to chapter 24)
- Share the bread and the wine, take communion together and remember the blood of the Lamb shed for you to keep you from being destroyed.
- Worship and praise Yah around the table with songs of thanksgiving and deliverance before the dessert.
- After the dessert go into a time of prayer.
- Pray for the salvation of Israel and of your nation, that they may come out of all slavery and bondage. Ask Yahveh to do miracles in this present time.
- Pray for the salvation of your family and for its deliverance.
- You can be creative and dramatize the story of the deliverance from Egypt and make an improvised theatre with the children present.
- Share a personal testimony on how God saved you and set you free.
- If there is someone that does not know Yeshua, this is a good time to lead them to salvation.
- Receive a special offering to advance the gospel in Israel and the nations!

More Scriptures to study: (Exodus 34:25, Numbers 9:2-14, Numbers 28:16, Numbers 33:3, Deuteronomy 16:1-

6, Joshua 5:10,11, 2 Kings 23:21, 2 Chronicles 30:1-18, 2 Chronicles 35:1-19, Ezra 6:19,20, Ezekiel 45:21, Matthew 26:2-19, Mark 14:1-16, Luke 2:41, Luke 22;1-15, John 2:13,23, John 6:4, John 11:55, John 12:1, John 13:1, John 18:28, John 18:39, John 19:14, 1 Corinthians 5:7, Hebrews 11:28)

Resurrection Day

This most important day, when Yeshua rose from the dead has been celebrated by Christians worldwide at the wrong date and with the pagan name of Easter. Yeshua rose from the dead three days and nights after His crucifixion. He was sacrificed on Preparation Day the 14th of Abib and He was put in the ground on Passover eve, the 15th of the month of Abib. (Remember that biblical days begin at sunset, so the 14th ends at sunset and the 15th begins at sunset!) He was in the ground on the 15th, 16th, 17th for 3 nights and in the ground for 3 days on the 16th, 17th, 18th. The 14th was a Wednesday. So, He spent Wednesday, Thursday, Friday nights buried, and Thursday, Friday and Saturday days buried. Before the night of Saturday at twilight He had to rise since He could not stay buried a fourth night! He rose some time at the end of Shabbat, right before Yom Rishon (The first day of the week which begins at sunset as all biblical days do!). He rose on Shabbat the 18th of the month of Abib! The number 18 in Hebrew letters is the word CHAY, which means LIFE! Since He rose at the end of Shabbat and at the outset of the First Day (Yom Rishon), He fulfilled both the Shabbat and the Feast of First Fruits. Remember that when I say "fulfill" I mean that He brought it to its *full* meaning and *not* that He abolished it!

He is our Shabbat (place of dwelling and rest) and He is the First Fruits of those raised from the dead.

"Now after the Sabbath, as it began to dawn toward the first day of the week, Mary Magdalene and the other Mary came to look at the grave."

— Matthew 28:1

Remember that the first day of Passover is a Shabbat or a holy convocation and is treated as a Shabbat. That is why the Word talks about Him being buried before the Shabbat, but it was not a weekly Shabbat, but the Passover Shabbat and they are both called Shabbat! On top of it, because many Jews lived outside of Israel due to the former exiles, it was, and still is, traditional to celebrate two Passover Shabbats of holy convocations, in order to allow for everyone throughout the earth to 'catch up.' So, at the time of Yeshua: Wednesday to Thursday was the first Passover Shabbat; Thursday to Friday was the second Passover Shabbat, and then Friday to Saturday night was the regular weekly Shabbat. That is why Mary Magdalene came to the tomb very early on the first day of the week in order to anoint His body with spices and found the tomb empty! The tomb however was already empty, before the following night; otherwise Yeshua would have been in the grave four nights instead of three.

However, Mary (Miriam) would have not been able to come to the grave until after Shabbat was over, and before the dawn of the first day of the week! (Remember that a biblical day begins at sun set). He rose as Shabbat ended! Which is perfectly in accordance with His finished work at the cross—then He entered into His rest and sat at the right hand of the Father. Saturday night is already considered the first day of the week. He rose right at the outset of the feast of first fruits, celebrated on the first day after the Shabbat! He is the first fruits of the resurrection.

(1 Corinthians 15:20, Matthew 28:1, John 20:1) He fulfilled three holy feasts—Death (Passover), Burial (Unleavened Bread), Resurrection (First Fruits)

Dispelling the Myth of Good Friday

Good Friday is not the correct commemoration of the crucifixion, because He was crucified on Passover eve and that was a Wednesday and was buried before sunset. This was one of the dates changed from the times of Constantine and the Council of Nicaea. In any case, the whole theory of Good Friday is farfetched since from Friday night to Sunday morning there are only two nights and not three nights as required! And only one day! Yeshua said that there would be only one sign, the sign of Jonah-which is three days and three nights in the belly of the earth! Many, many pogroms and massacres of Jewish People took place when Good Friday was being commemorated as the infuriated 'Christian Mob' would get out on mass to kill the Jews that killed Christ. (Matthew 12:39, 40, 16:4, Luke 11:29, 30)

From now on you can celebrate Passover and Resurrection Day at their proper times and with their holy names!

*Shabbat means to stop, to rest, *to sit* and to dwell! (From the Hebrew root *shevet*, meaning "to sit" or "to dwell.")

Feast of Weeks / Shavuot / Pentecost

(Numbers 28:26, Leviticus 23:15-21) This is also one of the three *regalim* or pilgrimage feasts where all male were required to show up before Yahveh in Jerusalem at the holy temple.

This celebration normally falls in the month of June. It is one day long, and it is called Feast of Weeks because seven weeks are counted from the Shabbat after the Feast of unleavened bread until this time of celebrations. On that day a first fruit offering of grain, particularly barley, is brought to Yahveh at the temple. This one-day feast is a Shabbat. The Book of Ruth is read at that time, since Ruth and Naomi arrived at Bethlehem at the beginning of the barley harvest (Ruth 2:22), which is the time of Shavuot. Also, according to rabbinical calculations, the Torah, Tablets of the Testimony, were given on Mount Sinai at the time of Shavuot.

Another important event happened during that time, 2000 years ago. The Jewish disciples of Messiah were waiting and praying in an upper room, celebrating Shavuot, when:

"Suddenly there came from heaven a noise like a violent rushing wind and it filled the whole house where they were sitting. And there appeared to them tongues as of fire distributing themselves, and they rested on each one of them. And they were all filled with the Holy Spirit and began to speak with other tongues as the Spirit gave them utterance."

— Acts 2:1-4

Remember that I explained that the Moadim are appointed times when Yah testifies of Himself and shows up? This is exactly what He did there. *He showed up* and baptized all these Jewish believers with the Holy Spirit and fire and they were transformed into vessels of glory!

Practical Applications

- Keep it as a special Shabbat (see Shabbat applications)
- Pray and wait on Yahveh for revival in Israel and in your nation.
- Pray for unity in the church and for all of it to be grafted into the olive tree.
- Pray for revival in your life and family.
- Read the Book of Ruth and pray that the church will be as Ruth to Israel.
- Make this Shabbat a Holy Spirit, prophetic night!
- Give a special offering to Yeshua from the best that you have.

The Fall Feasts – Trumpets, Atonement

(Leviticus 23:24-32) The Feast of Trumpets or of Shofars is a one-day feast or Shabbat. (Today it is celebrated for two days in Israel, because of the Jews in exile). The shofar or ram's horn is blown in all the synagogues and then from sunset to sunset a Shabbat is celebrated. One month prior to the Feast of Shofars, begins the month of repentance or forgiveness or in Hebrew—*Slichot*. It is the time to get right with your neighbor and with all people.

From the Feast of Shofars, also called in Hebrew *Yom Terua*, begins the countdown of the Ten Days of Awe, culminating with the most solemn day of the year, the Day of the Atonements or *Yom Hakippurim*, when the last trumpet-shofar is blown!

The Feast of Shofars is also called Rosh Hashanah, or the head of the year, and it is celebrated as the official Jewish New Year. This is a new year for civil affair The biblical new year is in the month of Abib, the month of Passover at spring time, which is the first month of the year. (See Exodus 12). The Feast of Shofars normally happens in September. The Hebrew date is the First of Tishrei or the first day of the seventh Hebrew month.

The Seven-Fold Purpose of the Shofar Blowing

The blowing of the Shofar carries much weight in the Spirit!

1. As an alarm in times of war (Numbers 10:9, Numbers 31:6, Jeremiah 4:19, Jeremiah 42:14,)
2. As a prophetic instrument to call to repentance (Leviticus 23, Joel 2)
3. As an instrument of judgment (Joshua 4, Revelation 8)
4. To gather the troops and the elect. (Judges 6:34, Matthew 24:31)
5. To declare victory. (Judges 7:18)
6. To send and loose the angels. (Matthew 24:31, Revelation 9:14,15)
7. To declare freedom, transformation and restoration. (Leviticus 25, 1 Corinthians 15:52)

Practical Applications

- Blow the shofar.
- Celebrate it as a Shabbat.
- This is a prophetic time of prayer for repentance and revival.
- In most Jewish homes, sweet foods and apples dipped in honey are put on the table as this is the official Jewish New Year.
- The Ten days of Awe that follow is a perfect time to search your heart and turn from any sin. This is a preparation for the Day of Atonement.

The Day of Atonement

(Leviticus 23:27-32, Numbers 29:7-11) On the 10th day of the seventh Hebrew month is the most solemn day of the biblical calendar. The whole nation was called to humble itself before Yah and afflict their souls through a total fast. It is the day that determined who lived and who died. It also determined the fate of the whole nation. During that day the high priest would enter into the holy of holies in the Temple. That was the place of the ark of the covenant and the mercy seat. That was the only residence and throne of the Most High on earth! The high priest could only come in after presenting a sin offering to atone for his and his family's sins, and another one for the whole of Israel. He would enter into the holy of holies with the blood and pour it on the mercy seat. If Yah received the sacrifice, He forgave the sin of the *entire* nation! If He did not, the high priest would die in the presence of Yahveh!

That is why the high priest had to confess and atone for his and his Sons' sins *first* and could not enter in without that atonement for himself! In the Talmud, the Jewish book of oral tradition and law, it is stated that there used to be right outside the holy of holies, a flax of wool died red. This flax of wool would turn completely white during Yom Hakippurim, when the high priest presented the blood before the throne as a sign of God's complete forgiveness, based on the following Scripture,

"Though your sins be as scarlet they shall be as white as snow; though they be red like crimson, they shall be as wool"

— Isaiah 1:18

I have heard that there was a time when that flax of wool did not turn white anymore when the atonement sacrifices were presented. That time was after Yeshua's death burial and resurrection, when He paid the price for sin, no more animals could do the job that He did so perfectly! The sacrifice of atonement used to cover the sins of Israel for only one year, the blood atonement of Yeshua has removed those sins altogether when one believes and trusts in Him!

In Israel on this day, *everything closes*! There are no cars on the streets, unless it is a police car or an ambulance. Even very young children try to fast. A large portion of the nation spends most of the day in the synagogues.

- This is a most solemn day of fasting, prayer and worship.
- The fast is a total fast without food or drink.
- The whole day is given to prayer *together* with other believers.
- Absolutely no work is to be done on this day.
- It is a perfect time for intercession for the salvation of Israel!
- It is a perfect time of prayer for repentance in the church, that she will be pure and holy, without spot or blemish!

- It is a perfect time to intercede and repent on behalf of the nations.
- At the end of the day, at sunset the shofar is blown. This is called 'The last trumpet" or the last shofar!

"In a moment in a twinkling of an eye, at the last trumpet; for the trumpet will sound, and the dead will be raised imperishable, and we will be changed."

— 1 Corinthians 15:52

Sukkoth – The Feast of Booths (Tabernacles)

(Leviticus 23: 34-43, Numbers 29:11-39) This is a most joyous season that is meant to remind us that we dwelt in booths or temporary dwellings in the desert prior to possessing the promised land. Thus, we realize that everything in life is temporary and frail. Only He is our habitation and the rock of our salvation. He is our permanent dwelling place!

It begins on the 15th day of the seventh Hebrew month (normally on September or October). The feast is celebrated for seven days, however on the eighth day there is a holy convocation (another Shabbat). Also, on the first day there is a holy convocation. So, there is a rest (Shabbat) on the first day and a rest (Shabbat) on the eighth day!

This is the exact season of the birth of Messiah. He was born at the Feast of Sukkoth not at Christmas time, (which is a pagan feast to the God Tammuz and celebrates the winter witchcraft solstice!) The calculations for Sukkoth are easy to make once you understand the priestly shifts and take into consideration the time when Miriam (Mary) fell pregnant and the time that Elizabeth fell pregnant with John. We must remember that these appointed times are the times when Yah shows up. Therefore, Messiah had to be born at one of these times, in the same way that He died and was resurrected at one of these appointed times. It is of great interest to note the following: The eighth day is the day when Jewish boys are circumcised. The eighth day of this feast is a holy convocation, a Shabbat, and it is the only biblical feast that has an eighth day! Yeshua was circumcised on the eighth day as He officially entered into the Covenant of Abraham, as a Jew!

The Feast of Sukkoth will be celebrated during the millennium and it will be *mandatory for the nations!* Those nations that do not come to Jerusalem to celebrate it will not have rain—*no blessing.* That is why many Christians come to Jerusalem during the Feast each year already before the Millennium!

"Then it will come about that any who are left of all nations that went against Jerusalem will go up from year to year to worship the King, Yahveh of the Armies, and to celebrate the Feast of Booths. And it will be that whichever of the families of the earth does not go up to Jerusalem to worship the King, Yahveh of the Armies, there will be no rain on them..."

— Zechariah 14:16-19

The Word says that there will be a plague to the nations that don't go!

"If the family of Egypt, does not go up or enter, then no rain will fall on them; it will be the plague with which Yahveh smites the nations that do not go up to celebrate the Feast of Booths."

— Zechariah 14:18

Yeshua was born in a humble manger, came to dwell in the frailty of a human body and has become our permanent Dwelling Place. In Him we live and move and have our being!

Yeshua was born in a humble manger, came to dwell in the frailty of a human body and has become our permanent dwelling place. In Him we live and move and have our being!

Sukkoth is a Latter Rain Feast and as such it is the feast of the last ingathering of the harvest. Yeshua mentioned, 'The fields being white, ready to be harvested', when He talked about Israel and the nations salvation. In Israel, right at the time of Sukkoth, is the cotton harvest, and before it is harvested it looks completely white!

Practical Applications

- Build in your yard or garden a temporary booth, a simple construction that has no roof. Make sure that you put palm branches, willows and other green leafy branches as the roof through which you can see the stars. Put a table, some chairs and maybe a bed in your *sukka* (*Booth*). Decorate it with Scriptures and drawings of agriculture, fruit and harvest.

- We are commanded to dwell in the Sukkah for seven days. To dwell can be, to sleep in it, to eat in it, to study in it and to spend some time in it. Some people live in it all the time and some others spend some time in it through the feast. Our favorite is eating meals in it and studying Torah and worshipping Yah.
- If you don't have a yard or a garden you can share a Sukkah with another family that does, or your church could build a big communal Sukkah.
- Some people build their booths indoors. However, it is not possible to see the sky through them.
- The first day, celebrate it as a Shabbat in the Sukkah.
- On the following days when you come from work you can eat a meal and pray there.
- This feast is of great joy and celebration. It is a great time to do high praise services and rejoice!
- It is an anointed time to pray for the harvest in Israel and the nations and to pray for the Father to send *more* laborers to the harvest!
- It is an important time to pray for the End time re-grafting of the church back into the olive tree!
- This is the right time to study the book of Exodus and the story of Yeshua's birth.
- If you don't have a yard or a garden you can share a Sukkah with another family that does, or your church could build a big communal Sukkah.
- Some people build their booths indoors. However, it is not possible to see the sky through them.

- If you don't have a yard or a garden you can share a Sukkah with another family that does, or your church could build a big communal Sukkah.
- Some people build their booths indoors. However, it is not possible to see the sky through them.
- The first day, celebrate it as a Shabbat in the Sukkah.
- On the following days when you come from work you can eat a meal and pray there.
- This feast is of great joy and celebration. It is a great time to do high praise services and rejoice!
- It is an anointed time to pray for the harvest in Israel and the nations and to pray for the Father to send *more* laborers to the harvest!
- It is an important time to pray for the End time re-grafting of the church back into the olive tree!
- This is the right time to study the book of Exodus and the story of Yeshua's birth.
- During the time of Nehemiah, they read the Torah, the whole book of the law (the Pentateuch or the five books of Moses) during the feast. The priests read it publicly. This is an excellent time to read the Torah out loud to your family and congregation!
- On the eighth day it is a holy convocation, a, a time of rejoicing over the giving of the law. Remember that Yeshua is the Word made flesh; He is the law, the Torah made flesh! And we rejoice that He was born as a Jew and entered into the covenant of Abraham on the eighth day!

- If for any reason you cannot build a Sukkah, by all means celebrate the first and the eighth days as Shabbats, holy convocations and high praise services with your family and with your congregation! Make it a point to remember to meditate on His law, His Torah, during the feast week. Also remember Jerusalem and Israel in your prayers for revival!

- At each of these *Moadim* that you are beginning to celebrate, do not forget to allow the precious Holy Spirit to guide you and show you how to work them it in your particular situation in your culture and nation.

- Make it a point to come to Jerusalem to celebrate the Feast with us. Check our website for details on that: www.zionsgospel.com.

- Organize Sukkoth Feasts in your congregations or nations; contact our ministry for details.

Special insight

At the time of Sukkoth, Yeshua's birth, the shepherds were in the field in a Sukkah and saw the sky and the angels in heaven announcing the *good news*!

CHAPTER TWELVE:
Holy Diet

Creational Statutes Numbers 2 & 3

"You shall take with you of every clean animal by sevens, a male and his female; and of the animals that are not clean two, a male and his female."

— Genesis 7:2

Number Two

Already in Genesis seven, we read that Noah brought into the ark, two by two of the unclean or impure animals and seven by seven of the clean and the pure animals. All of Leviticus 11 is still for today. The animals have never changed! It is still not acceptable for a believer in the holy God of Israel to consume those animals that He called unclean.

Number Three

The statute connected with consuming blood. This is a creational principle, in Leviticus 17:10-14 we learn that the 'life of the flesh is in the blood' and already in Genesis 9:4— *"Only you shall not eat flesh with its life that is its blood"*

Sometimes when I teach people about the dietary Commandments according to Leviticus 11, they show signs of discomfort. They think that I am trying to 'put them under the law.' My dear friends the opposite is the truth! I am endeavoring to show you the ways of the blessing and the way out of endless sickness, disease and a host of other problems. You see I know my Father in heaven and He is *good.* He is not 'sometimes good and sometimes not.' He is all good! His purpose from the beginning was to give us the best. That is what Adam had. He had the best heaven could offer, right here on earth. And when they disobeyed one dietary Commandment and they ate from the forbidden tree, they lost everything! That dietary Commandment was for their own good. Elohim knew that that tree was bad for them. He created that tree that way; but the snake lied to them and basically said that the tree was actually good for them, and that Elohim was not good because He did not want them to enjoy themselves. Even today the same snake is lying to most Christians, making them believe that the Torah is bondage and that the dietary laws are not for today.

Would a good father or mother give to his child food filled with worms? Would a good father feed his child with food that kills them before their time and causes damage to the brain and internal organs? I surely think that no good parent would kill their children intentionally with that kind of food! Do you think that a good parent would tell a child a lie? Something like this: 'You are free to eat this food filled with worms as long as you bless it.' Then the child would believe his or her parent and take that food with thanksgiving and then become sick and die prematurely and even get epileptic seizures? Can you imagine a scenario like that? Would that child trust his or her parent again? I don't think so! However, the majority of the church has been made to believe this lie and to misinterpret many Scriptures in the Torah and to make the God of Israel a liar.

I have been a nutritionist and a health consultant for over 20 years now and I can assure you that science itself proves the Word of God true about all the dietary laws as written in Leviticus 11.

Science has proven pigs to be one of the deadliest, poisoning and disease promoting animals that people ingest. In an article entitled, 'Death in the Kitchen', by A. N. Dugger, the editor of the Mt. Zion reporter, it reads:

The United States Medical Association has sent out many broadcasts warning about the danger of eating swine's flesh. A post mortem examination showed Trichina in the bodies of 75% of dead people over 60 years of age, in a certain large city of America, and this city was not exceptional. Others were supposed to rate just as high.

All pork (swine's flesh) is infested with a small serpent-like worm, so small that they cannot be seen without a strong magnifying glass. These worms are called 'Trichina.' In different ways when pork is eaten, they get into the human body, and lodge in some organs, bring on a diseased condition and death, which occurs sometimes after a few months or weeks, and sometimes causes a lingering illness.

One writer describes the case of a sufferer in these words—"An intelligent lady, a teacher in the public schools, who died of this horrible disease in consequence of tasting a single mouthful of uncooked sausage, said to the writer as she was panting for breath, after suffering untold agonies from myriads of those horrible parasites which were working their way through every fiber of her body": Warn people not to eat pork!" These little worms get into the blood stream and are carried to all parts of the body. If they set up their breeding quarters in any organ, that person dies of that disease without its cause being mentioned. It has been claimed by medical authorities in the US that 50% of the deaths of people over 30 are caused by this infection.

It is said that cooking thoroughly, will destroy the larva and the eggs, but they have been found to be fertile after rendering the lard from the fat. (Not even high heat cooking destroys them! D.B.) *The lard is the fat.

Some people say: "...But I have enough faith and if I pray over them and bless the pork it will become 'clean' and will not harm me."

Unfortunately, that is not really scriptural and countless Christians are praying and 'blessing' pork every day and they are still sick with many diseases connected with blood dishes, pork, shellfish, shrimps and other 'unclean delicacies.' In fact some of the sickest people are actually in the church!

See the following passage of Scripture:

"For every creature of God is good, and nothing is to be refused if it is received with thanksgiving' for it is sanctified *by the Word of God and prayer.*"

— 1 Timothy 4:4-5

Please note that there are two things that will sanctify your food:

1. The Word of God
2. Prayer

Prayer Alone Does Not Sanctify Your Food. The Word Is Needed Also.

When the New Testament speaks about *the Word* it always means the Tanach or commonly called the Old Testament Scriptures. Their real name is the holy Scriptures. At the time that Saul/Paul the Apostle, emissary of Yeshua, wrote this letter to Timothy, there was no New Testament portion of the bible. This was canonized only 300 years later! There is not one Scripture in the Holy Scriptures, the Tanach, that sanctifies blood, pork or shrimp or any of the unclean animals described in Leviticus 11 (please read the chapter). On the contrary there are many Scriptures connecting swine with curses and with idolatry.

Look at this prophetic word in Isaiah 66 about the End times. In the New King James English bible, it is entitled:

true worship and false. *"For by fire and by His sword the Lord will judge all flesh; and the slain of the Lord will be many. Those who sanctify themselves and purify themselves to go to the gardens after an idol in the midst,* eating swine's flesh and the abomination and the mouse, shall be consumed together," says the Lord.

Here the Word is clearly connecting idolatrous practices with the eating of unclean animals. It is very revealing that Yeshua cast the demons out of the demoniac from Gadarenes into a herd of pigs. Why did He not choose sheep or goats for that?

He always intended for pigs and all unclean animals to serve the purpose of 'garbage collectors', both spiritual and physical. They all eat garbage or rotten flesh. You and I are children of the king of kings and we deserve a lot better than this!

To sanctify, means to make it holy for holy use! Have you ever thought that you are holy? You and I are the very temple of the Holy Spirit, so Elohim intends even your food to be holy, your children to be holy, and your finances to be holy? The holy lifestyle is the lifestyle of the blessing!

"And a highway shall be there, and a way and it shall be called the way of holiness; the unclean shall not pass over it, but it shall be for others. Whoever walks the road though a fool shall not go astray."

— Isaiah 35:8

This Scripture tells us that anyone who wants to walk in obedience to the blessing, the way of the holy Commandments, and the way of Torah as revealed by the Spirit, can do it. You don't have to be a super person! The Holy Spirit has come for this very purpose, to help us walk in the way of the blessing that is the highway of holiness!

I am completely aware that when you decide to enter into the blessing of Abraham, in its fullness you have some choices to make, some decisions to take and that is why Yah said to the people of Israel:

"I call heaven and earth as witnesses today against you, that I have set before you, life and death, blessing and cursing; therefore, choose life, that both you and your descendants may live."

— Deuteronomy 30:19

It is all about life and blessing, abundant life and that is what YHVH intended when He gave the Commandments to Israel and when He walked the earth in the form of Messiah Yeshua and when He sent the Holy Spirit to write the Torah in our hearts and to help us interpret it. May this life and blessing, health and prosperity be yours as you restore to you and to your family that which the devil has stolen and lied about for so long, The Torah interpreted by the Ruach, the Spirit of Elohim.

An Important Deliverance Prayer

Dear Father in heaven, thank You for being all good and wanting to bless me in every area of my life. Forgive me for not fully believing in Your goodness and for wrongly thinking that Your holy instructions, called Torah, were to put me in bondage or to steal my salvation 'freedom.' I understand today that true freedom is to be healthy, holy and blessed and that You have given to me instructions in Your Holy Hebrew Scriptures that can teach me the lifestyle of the blessing. Please keep on revealing this subject to me. I also renounce any addiction I may have to unclean animals, including pork and shellfish and to blood dishes. I only want to be addicted to You and to Your Word. I break the power of any addiction and I am willing to let you write Your Torah completely in my heart. I renounce all unnecessary fear and I bind every spirit of fear that I have had concerning the Torah, and I ask the Holy Spirit to teach it to me now. In Yeshua's name I pray, amen.

Important Notice

Please read Leviticus 11 thoroughly and find out what are the animals and fish in your own country that is unclean.

Practical Applications

- Check if the fish you eat has scales and fins. Do not eat just any fish. (Catfish is unclean fish)

- All shellfish is unclean. This includes all oysters, shrimp, crab, octopus, etc.

- When you order in a restaurant be very specific and *clear*. Tell them that you want no pork, bacon, ham, bacon bits, pork seasoning, oyster or fish sauce, etc...

- Do not be ashamed to return a dish if you need to. In most countries, the waiters are very ignorant about food matters.

- Do not have the fear of men. Be faithful to your convictions.

- In most countries, lard or animal fat and gelatin are made from pork.

- In many countries, even a house salad, comes on a bed of ham. Be specific and display strength of character.

- Remember that we were not called to be the 'sugar of the earth' but the 'salt of the earth.' Do not fear the opinions of men!

- Get rid of any unclean 'food' in your refrigerator. Maybe the cats or the dogs will eat it. However, if you love your pet, you might want to give him something more wholesome!

- If you make a mistake and you eat something that you did not mean to, just ask Yah to cleanse you from its effects and poison. In this case the Scripture mentioned in Mark 16:18 can be of great effect: *"If they drink a deadly poison, it will not hurt them"* If you drink or eat anything deadly or profane, by mistake, Yah's Word will protect you. However, if you drink it or eat it on purpose, this is a way of putting God to the test. Yeshua quoted that to Satan in the desert.

"Yeshua said unto him, 'It is written, you shall not put the Lord Your God to the test."

— Matthew 4:7

- If you think that dietary statutes are not important, take a good look at Genesis 3 and see what the breaking of *one* dietary law caused to all mankind!
- Anyone that quotes Paul to you, please ask them to read my entire book or challenge them to read Matthew 5:17-20, Romans 2:1-16, Jeremiah 31:31-34. Explain kindly to them that they have been fed misinterpretations of the New Testament through a replacement theology gospel.
- Remember that you are saved by putting your faith in the finished work of Yeshua at the cross, and then you are born again and begin to walk in obedience to Yah's ways as the Holy Spirit writes them in your heart. The Word says, *"Ask and it shall be given unto you."* As you ask the Holy Spirit, He will give you His revelation and write His laws in your heart. He will lead you into all truth if you let Him!
- Remember that the good news is for the humble. Understanding the blessing of the dietary laws is for the humble. Those are the ones that will be strong,

healthy and holy enough to be great and to be filled with Yah's glory!

"May Your compassion come to me that I may live, for Your law is my delight"

— Psalm 119:77

CHAPTER THIRTEEN:
Holy Finances

Creational Statutes Numbers 4 & 5

"Honor the Lord from your wealth and from the first of all your produce. So, your barns will be filled with plenty and your vats will overflow with new wine."

— Proverbs 3:9, 10

Number Four

The laws of first fruits is already implied in Genesis 4, when Cain brought an offering (any offering) to Elohim and Abel brought the *first* of his flock. The offering of Abel was accepted but that of Cain was not! The reason is that Cain did not bring a first fruit offering like he should have! Abel obeyed the statute and brought a first fruit offering.

Number Five

The laws of tithes already appear in the Book of Genesis when Abraham gave Malchizedek, the king of Salem, (Genesis 14: 19, 20) a tithe of all that he had.

Creation Torah

The Law of First Fruits

"So, it came about in the course of time that Cain brought an offering to the Lord of the fruit of the ground. Abel on his part also brought of the firstlings of his flock and of their fat portion. And the Lord had regards for Abel and for his offering. But for Cain and for his offering He had *no regard.*"

The Word of God tells us that Yahveh, the Lord, is a just and righteous judge. So, when we see Him seemingly 'respecting persons' as in this case, we need to ask ourselves what was it that displeased Yah to the point that He had no regard for Cain's offering? What was it that pleased Him so that He had regard for Abel's offering?

We read in Hebrews 11:6 that *without faith it is impossible to please God* and that *He is a rewarder of them that diligently seek Him.* In the Book of Jacob 2:14-17 (James) we read that *faith without works is dead* and that faith can be shown by works. We can see that for some reason Cain's offering was not an act of faith and was not pleasing, thus his work was not acceptable before the Creator.

In Deuteronomy 28:1-14 we read that when we hear and do (*Shma*) what Yah tells us to do, when we keep His revealed Commandments, He blesses us and exalts us above others. In other words, He is not expecting us to act without His guidance and without knowledge of His ways and when we do, it is not acceptable. He does not accept any offering; He only accepts perfect offerings given with a perfect heart.

In the Book of Malachi, we read:

"You also say, 'my how tiresome it is!' And you disdainfully sniff at it, says the Lord of hosts, "and you bring what was taken by robbery and what is lame or sick; so you bring the offering! Should I receive it from your hand?" says the Lord? "But cursed be the swindler who has a male in his flock and vows it but sacrifices a blemished animal to the Lord. But I AM a great King. Says the Lord of hosts."

— Malachi 2:13, 14

In other words, YHVH does not accept faulty offerings and Cain's was a faulty offering, thus it was not acceptable. The reaction of Cain was typical of a man that is full of self-righteousness, one that is 'doing a favor to God by bringing Him anything at all.' His reaction was anger, lethal anger, followed by jealousy. All self-righteous people who think that they are good because they 'do for God' according to their own desires, get angry when you contest their 'goodness.' It is not enough to be 'good in our own estimation'; we need to be acceptable in God's eyes. And as I said before, only faith pleases Him, and obedient works that are an outcome of true faith. True faith takes Yah's instructions and follows them as He reveals them to us. A self -righteous man, 'figures out' what to do 'for God' in order to 'look good' in the eyes of others and in his own eyes. Self -righteousness does not seek to please God really, only to 'feel good about oneself.' All self -righteous acts are utterly selfish and utterly unacceptable! Only the Creator knows the heart of His creation and He definitely knew the heart of Cain. It was selfish, jealous and self-righteous. It was the heart of an unbeliever, thus he offered what he offered!

But what did he offer that was rejected? We need to understand that this was *the first* recorded offering ever brought to Elohim, God. In other words, this was a *first fruits offering*! We read here that Cain brought an offering. What does that mean? That he brought whatever he wanted but not what is commanded or prescribed. In the following verse we see that Abel's offering was a *first fruits* offering.

He brought the firstlings of his flock which of course was accepted!

"You shall devote to the Lord the *first offspring* of every womb and the first offspring of every beast that you own; the males belong to the Lord"

— Exodus 13:12

"That you shall take some of the *first of all the produce* of the ground which you bring in from your land that the Lord Your God gives you, and you shall put it in a basket and go to the place where the Lord Your God chooses to establish His name."

— Deuteronomy 26:2

"The first of the *first fruits* of your land you shall bring into the house of the Lord Your God."

— Exodus 23:19

"Honor the Lord from your wealth and from the *first* of all your produce. So, your barns will be filled with plenty and your vats will overflow with new wine."

— Proverbs 3:9-10

Cain did not honor Elohim with the first fruits of the ground; he just brought 'an offering.' Abel brought the firstlings of the flock. He honored the Creator and the Creator honored him. Obeying in offering correctly unto God is a faith issue; it is a heart issue. Both Cain and Abel were well aware of the laws of the Creator! Mount Sinai's Torah had not been given yet, and Israel did not exist yet as a people (Except in the heart of Yah!); however, His eternal Torah was already known on the earth and He was expecting men to follow it and please Him by faith and obedience! Cain knew how to do well but he chose not to.

"So, Cain became very angry and his countenance fell. Then the Lord said to Cain: Why are you angry and why is your countenance fallen? If you do well will not your countenance be lifted up? And if you do not do well, sin is crouching at the door, and its desire is for you, but you must master it."

— Genesis 4:6-7

The Creator expected Cain to do well, for He knew that Cain was well aware of His creation Torah and the laws off first fruits. Again, we can see that when we know to do well and we choose not to, it is sin! It is an outcome of a wicked heart and eventually it leads to worse sins. In this case Cain sinned by not bringing his first fruits offering. Then he sinned again by not accepting Elohim's correction, and eventually he sinned by murdering his brother! This is exactly what happened when the Gentile portion of the church divorced from the Jews and the Torah, the Jewish roots of the faith. It began with defiling the Shabbat and the Passover and it continued with defiling the temple of the Holy Spirit with unclean animals. Finally, it culminated in murder of Jewish people, horrible pogroms, the Spanish Inquisition in the name of Christ, and the Holocaust. Today that spirit of Cain is working through Islam as well.

Special Prayer

The spirit of Cain has been in the church since its divorce from the Jews and the Jewish Roots of the Faith, as it has rejected Yah's laws and Commandments and rejected the Jews. Let us pray that the spirit of Cain will be cast out of the church worldwide; that the church will decide to receive correction from the Master and will not react like Cain, with anger and more murder. Let us pray that the church will humble her heart and be willing to go through the transformation necessary in order to be delivered of all anti-Mesitojuz and to be restored to the original Apostolic, Jewish foundations of the faith, thus becoming the *best* friend of Messiah, and the *best* friend that Israel has ever had, in these end of times. Let us also pray for the spirit of Cain to break off the Moslems, so they can be saved and embrace the Jewish Messiah!

Therefore, to him that knows to do good and does it not. To him it is sin.

— James 4:17.

The first fruits offerings need to be given unto the priests, those that minister the Word:

"Speak to the Sons of Israel and say to them; 'when you enter the land which I am going to give to you and reap its harvest, then you shall bring in the sheaf of the first fruits of your harvest to the priest. Until this same day, until you have brought in the offering of Your God, you shall eat neither bread nor roasted grain for new growth. It is to be a perpetual statute throughout your generations in all your dwelling places."

— Leviticus 23:10, 14

The first fruits offerings are so important, that the Word instruct the people *not to even eat* until they have brought these offerings to the priest, so that he and his family could eat! When is the last time that you delayed your own meal until you brought your pastor or another minister of the gospel your best portion? When is the last time that you delayed your shopping of a new car or a house until you brought a suitable offering so that another minister of the gospel or your own pastor could buy his/her car or house? It is very important that you take care of the priests that are ministering the Word to you *before* you take care of your own house and family.

"You look for much but behold it comes to little, when you bring it home, I blow it away. Why? Declares the Lord of hosts, "Because of My house which lies desolate, while each of you runs to his own house."

— Haggai 1:9

This same principle we see when Elijah told the widow of Sarepta to give him *first* and *then* the widow would have a supernatural supply for her and her son during the time of drought! (1 Kings 17).

I believe that every member of the body should make sure that their five-fold ministry leaders, from which they receive ministry, be fully supplied and blessed! And not only those that minister directly in their congregation, but also those that minister to them through their writings and media program. Those that are preaching the gospel and advancing the Kingdom.

I believe that if you have a minister that is blessing your life through his/her ministry and you do nothing to bless them, it is serious ignorance! It is true that some preachers have abused this gift; however, most of them are working hard and doing their best to minister to God's people. It would be good for you to do a heart inspection in this matter, as many people are offended by the thought of giving to a servant of Yah. As if they are expecting that God will make money grow on trees for them! Not so, beloved! The Word instructs us to take care of Yah's house first, and His house is built as the Apostles, Prophets, Evangelists, Teachers and Pastors speak and teach His Word, His truth. (Ephesians 4:11-15)

An Important Fact

Even in your giving you need to apply the eternal principle—to the Jew first.

"For I am not ashamed of the gospel of Messiah: For it is the power of God unto salvation to everyone that believes to the Jew first."

— Romans 1:16

"But honor glory and peace to every man that worketh good, to the Jew first and also to the Gentile."

— Romans 2:10 KJV

In other words, we need to honor and bless the Jews and Israel first and then all the rest will be honored and blessed. Remember that Yah is a God of order and He is *very* particular about His order! Every congregation should have a project to support Israel and Jewish ministers first. Thus. the blessing of Abraham would fall on many!

"I will bless those who bless thee...And in thee all the families of the earth will be blessed."

— Genesis 12:3

The Poor Man's Portion

"When you reap the harvest of your land, moreover you shall not reap to the very corners of your field, nor gather the gleaning of your harvest; you are to leave them for the needy and the alien. I AM Yahveh your Elohim"

— Leviticus 23:22

The Father instructs us here to always leave something for the poor. You may not have a field, but you do get wages, and His instruction is to always consider the poor. However, to the poor we are not instructed to give the *best*, the *tithe* or the *first fruits*. Those are to be given to the priests! Today in the body of Messiah, most people are giving the priests the 'poor man's portion.' They give the ministers whatever they have left! This is a very serious issue that has *devalued* the Word of God and the importance of the ministry of the Word and Spirit! The residues and leftovers are for the poor. The first and choicest offerings are for the priests. When you honor Yah in His servants, the spirit of poverty is defeated and the

Word of Yah is exalted and begins to manifest richly; and so is the power and anointing of the Holy Spirit! This is the reason for the lack of anointing and glory. We have treated the ministers of the Word as beggars instead of holding them in high esteem. We must repent of this!

The principle is very simple and clear:

If you give your best to the poor, you exalt poverty. If you give your best to the ministers of the Word, you exalt Yah's Word!

Giving the residues to the poor is an act of *mercy*. Giving the first and best to the priest is an act of *honor*! When we treat the priests as beggars and give them the leftovers, it is an act of shame and dishonor. So, let us have *mercy* over the poor and *honor* the ministers of the Word!

Life Application

Begin to ask the Father to write this law of the first fruits in your heart. Today most people are not shepherds or farmers. Most people receive wages or have their own business. How can you apply the law of first fruits and please God with your offerings? I suggest that you separate the *first* day of every month as your offering day. Whatever you earn on that first day monthly is your first fruits offering. If you receive wages, besides taking the tithe out, divide your paycheck into 28 working days and that portion is your first fruits on top of the tithe. If you are in business, the first sale of the month, give it unto the Lord, but don't exchange it, otherwise it will bring a curse to you. You can send your first fruits offering to whatever minister of the Word that Yah will instruct you. It will normally be a ministry that is obeying the Father. Maybe when you do your monthly shopping, you will separate the first and best and take it as an offering to your minister. Pray and He will show you. Please notice that these are only suggestions on how to apply the first fruits principle. You have to seek Yah for yourself according to your own situation. The important thing is that from now on you will be very mindful as to what you give as an offering. Always seek Him and endeavor to do your best to honor His servants!

Common Questions

- *Do I have to give first fruits offerings?* Elohim does not want anything from you unless you desire to give it with a cheerful heart and with faith. Remember only faith can please God! (2 Corinthians 9:7)

- *Is this law for today?* According to Jeremiah 31:31-34, Matthew 5:17-20 it definitely is! The First Fruits Principle is eternal.

- *What will happen if I don't obey it?* If you know to do good and you do not, to you it is sin. You will definitely be missing the blessings of God. Also, it shows me that you have a lukewarm walk. When our walk is 'on fire' we are full of faith and are willing to do all that He tells us to do! See Revelation 3:14-15.

- *What if I do not have a heart conviction about it?* Then pray about it and let the Holy Spirit talk to you and instruct you personally. "As for you, the anointing which you received from Him abides in you; but as His anointing teaches you about all things and is true and is not a lie. And just as it has taught you, you abide in Him" 1 John 2:27. In other words, allow the Holy Spirit to become your Torah teacher and confirm what I have written in here and maybe give you more instruction!

- Since most of us are not in agriculture or have livestock, we must be led by the Spirit as to what would be a first fruits offering in our modern-day society. Example: When I print my books, the first box or package of books is my first fruits offering. However, it could also be my first book of the total edition. You must do what Yah's Spirit puts in your heart.

Remember the blessings promised to those that honor Yah with their first fruits,

"Honor the Lord from your wealth and from the *first* of all your produce. So, your barns will be filled with plenty and your vats will overflow with new wine."

— Proverbs 3:9-10

This is both a financial promise and a spiritual promise. As you follow this principle, you will have plenty for your needs financially and also spiritually as new wine is likened many times unto the Holy Spirit (Ephesians 5:18). I have no doubt that as you honor God's servants with your best, Yah will honor you with His best and your anointing will increase as well as your wealth!

Meditate on this word and let faith arise in your Spirit. Prosperity is at hand for the honorable and obedient!

The Law of Tithes

This is a very misunderstood and abused law in most churches. Many people are very disappointed nowadays as they have been promised by preachers that if they give their tithes, then they will be rich instantly. This Commandment is connected with *honor* and the holy, healthy fear and trust of Yah. The honorable way will eventually lead us to Shalom, wholeness and prosperity as we diligently *do* His Holy Word; however, it is not instant.

Obedience to this Commandment separates the idolaters from the Yah worshippers. Some trust the God of Mammon and their own abilities, rather than the God of Israel, to be their provider! Though obedience to God's Commandments and instructions will always lead to prosperity and blessing. When we tithe it is not the riches that we are pursuing, but rather it is an act of *honor*. We choose to honor Yah as our source and provision!

The purpose of the tithes is to provide sustenance to the ministers of God, those that dedicate their lives to teach and preach His Word. Tithes are the inheritance of the Levites and it is holy for that purpose. (Numbers 10:24, Numbers 18:26, Leviticus 27:30, 2 Chronicles 31:6)

Today it is the same, tithes should be given to those that minister the Word of God to you and to those that are dedicated to full time ministry, and they should share with those in their team. This principle is clearly stated in the New Testament or Apostolic Writings,

"The one who is taught the Word is to share all good things with the one who teaches him. Do not be deceived, God is not mocked; for whatever a man sows, this he will also reap."

— Galatians 6:6, 7

Abraham gave tithes to Malchizedek, because this priest had the ability to bless him (Genesis 14:18-20). Therefore, your tithes need to go into the hands of those ministers of the gospel that bless your life through their teaching and spiritual impartation. When you honor these servants with your tithes, it is the Almighty Himself that you are honoring. You are placing *value* on His Word and His Spirit flowing through His choice vessels! Tithing and first fruits giving to the ministers of Yah is an act of *honor* to Him and it releases the anointing from within these servants to minister to you! The Word says, 'Do not be deceived. God is not mocked.' Many are mocking Yahveh by not blessing His servants with their tithes and offerings. Then they do not understand why their spiritual growth is stunted!

192 ■ Grafted In

"Whatever a man sows, that will he reap." (Galatians 6:7)

If you sow dishonor to God by overlooking His servants and not honoring them and providing for them, you will have a very miserable harvest.

There is so much deception in this area in the body of Messiah. Once I had a mistaken Apostle in Latin America cancel a meeting on me because I taught by radio about this principle of honoring God by giving to the servants of Elohim! In a phone conversation with him, he was trying to force me to agree with him, that I was not trusting Yah for my provision, because I was expecting the church to provide for me! My dear people, this is what happens when we have no Torah in our hearts. Yah's instructions are *so* clear that it is His design and will that the people of God will minister financially to the servants of God who are feeding them. Anything else is a gross error! During the times of Elijah, for a season Elohim sent ravens to feed the prophet, but when the brook dried, He sent His prophet to a widow woman for sustenance. Though ravens might bring provision to prophets or other ministers of God, His first choice is that His people bless and provide for His servants! God had to use ravens because Israel was in thorough apostasy and they were following the prophets of Baal, so they were not tithing or giving offerings into Yah's true servants anymore. (1 Kings 17)

We really need to repent of this issue, for withholding the tithe, the first fruits and all the appointed offerings from the ministers of the Most High. This is a sign of apostasy and it has very negative effects throughout the church. When the Word of God in His servants, is not honored it brings terrible shame and dishonor to YHVH-Yeshua's holy name!

When people in the world are willing to support their rock and pop bands and their 'Lyon's Club' and Masonic lodges more than the people of God are willing to support, with their tithes and offerings, the ministers of His Holy Word, it is a disgrace to the Kingdom of God!

Let Us Pray

Dear Father in heaven, please forgive me for dishonoring Your Word and Your Spirit by not giving my tithes, first fruits and offerings to Your chosen servants who are preaching and teaching Your Word. I repent from my mistaken ways and I determine to begin to honor Your Word, Your Spirit and Your servants right away! In Yeshua's name. Amen.

Tithes are a kind of first fruit offering, but it is a specific percentage that Yah requires here, namely a ten percent of your income. Since it is taken from the top, before you pay your bills or the income tax, it is also a type of first fruits as it is your *top ten*.

The following is one of the most misquoted and misunderstood Scriptures in the bible.

"Bring the whole tithe into the storehouse, so that there may be food in my house, and test me now in this," says the Lord of hosts, "If I will

not open for you the windows of heaven and pour out for you a blessing until it overflows."

— Malachi 3:10

Most preachers that speak on tithes explain to the people that every time they give their tithes, God will open the windows of heaven and will flood them with blessings! And when it does not happen every time, they feel cheated, deceive and they quit tithing.

In some cases, they feel so cheated that they leave the church altogether! The reason is that this Scripture is taken out of context and with a thorough misunderstanding of its background. In this case YHVH was speaking to apostate Israel.

They had turned aside to idols and to immorality and they were far from God. Therefore, they did not care anymore about the work of the temple and about the sustenance of the priests. Elohim wanted to draw His people that were very alienated from Him back to His arms again, so He gave them a 'carrot': *Since you are so deceived, I want to prove to you that I AM real, and that obedience is the key for your blessing!* He was willing to do an instant miracle for them so that they would believe in Him. However, not in every situation when you tithe you will see dramatic effects in your finances. This was a particular case and it needed a dramatic effect, the opening of the windows of heaven instantly, so that His people would repent. Even today when someone is really far from God and they are new in the faith, He will give them dramatic results and instant results! But for most of us, He will require *long-term* faithfulness.

"The hand of the diligent will rule, but the slack hand will be put to forced labor."

— Proverbs 12:24

"Who will render to each person according to his deeds. To those who by perseverance in doing good seek for glory and honor and immortality, eternal life; but to those who are selfishly ambitious and do not obey the truth, but obey unrighteousness, wrath and indignation."

— Romans 2:6-8

Perseverance and diligent obedience to Yah's laws, Commandments and instructions is a lifestyle and a lifelong commitment. Eventually, after you have proven your faithfulness, He promises to reward you and prosper you. Too many people grow weary because they do not get instant results. The lifestyle of the Kingdom and its rewards is a *lifelong process*. It requires faithfulness, perseverance and diligence. It is like running a marathon. If you quit running after the first few meters, you will never reach your goal which is arriving at the finishing line and winning the marathon. If you get disappointed after a few minutes, you are a looser! As you serve God patiently and diligently, you will see His blessings come into your life gradually. One day you will look back and see where you came from and will realize that He has blessed you and He has rewarded you. Have long term faith in Yah and in His Word!

"And without faith it is impossible to please Him, for he who comes to God must believe that He is and that He is a rewarder of them that diligently seek Him."

— Hebrews 11:6 KJV

May the curse of dishonor and poverty that has come upon you be broken; and may you be restored to honor as you honor Yah and His servants with your tithes and offerings! May you become diligent and persistent in your obedience.

CHAPTER FOURTEEN:
No Mixture!

Creational Law Number Six

"You are to keep my statutes." You shall not breed together two kinds of your cattle; you shall not sow your field with two kinds of seed, nor wear a garment upon you of two kinds of material (natural fibers) mixed together."

— Leviticus 19:19

This is the law about *no mixture*. Elohim created all plants, animals and humans according to their kind. That is why a crossing between a horse and a donkey breeds a mule and a mule cannot reproduce! That is why God did not create transvestites and homosexuals. He created a man to be a man and a woman to be a woman. Every crossing of kinds is contrary to God's creational law and it causes confusion, pain and curses. *(See Genesis chapter one!)*

The God of Israel is a holy God and He tolerates no mixture. The most prevalent outcome of replacement theology since its inception in the second century by Origen is the ungodly tolerance and encouragement of mixture, both in our traditions, feasts, liturgies and life style.

See below what the Apostle Paul has to say about mixture,

"Do not be bound together with unbelievers; for what partnership have righteousness and lawlessness, or what fellowship has light with darkness? Or what harmony has Messiah with Belial, or what has a believer in common with an unbeliever? Or what agreement has the temple of God with idols? For we are the temple of the living God; just as God said, I will dwell and walk among them; and I will be their God, and they shall be my people; Therefore, come out from their midst and be separate, says YHVH. And do not touch what is unclean; and I will welcome you, and I will be a Father to you, and you shall be Sons and daughters to me, says the Lord Almighty."

— 2 Corinthians 6:14-17

These Scriptures reveal the heart of Paul for holiness and his love of Torah. Most of the laws and statutes in the Torah, deal with the importance of separation between the *holy* and the *profane*. In Ezekiel 44:15-24, we read about the Zadok priesthood, *"But the Levitical priests, the Sons of Zadok, who kept the charge of my sanctuary when the Sons of Israel went astray from me, shall come near to me, to minister to me... Moreover, they shall teach my people the difference between the holy and the profane, and cause them to discern between the unclean and the clean..."*

Even today, there is a Zadok like priesthood that is being brought near to Yah and they are being anointed for End time purposes! They will help the Ecclesia come out of the mixture and the profane replacement theology gospel into Yah's holiness and the gospel of the Kingdom. These Zadok like priests, men and women (many of them are women!) have a very delicate sense of smell, spiritually. Their discernment is very fine, and they do not tolerate mixture. Many people call them, 'radical', 'religious', 'exaggerated'; however, they are *holy* and preach *holiness*! Be careful not to come against one of them, or take them lightly as they are *anointed* by Yahveh for a very special, delicate and challenging task:

To take the church out of Babylon into Jerusalem!

They are Apostolic/Prophetic, and they are sent to the church to lead a move of holiness that tolerates *no mixture*! These have been forged in the fire of afflictions for many years in order to make them obedient, with no fear of man, bold as a lion yet loving and merciful. Their preparation has been long and very meticulous and Yah is very zealous over them. They are *his possession* for this urgent End time purpose—*restore the Ecclesia to her original Apostolic, Jewish foundations and to Holiness!* They carry an enormous weight of glory and spiritual authority and many of them are backed up with Apostolic/Prophetic signs, wonders and miracles. They do not caress the ears but express *truth* with clarity.

Many of them are extremely creative and will use sanctified arts to express the message!

One day I asked the Father, why He was using so many women in these End times? To which He replied to me:

Because they are better house cleaners, and I want My house clean!

So, many of these third day, third millennium apostles and prophets are women and they are sent to the body, to the church, so the bride, the New Jerusalem can come forth! And the New Jerusalem tolerates no mixture either!

"And the city has no need of the sun or of the moon to shine on it, for the glory of God has illumined it, and its lamp is the lamb... And nothing unclean, and no one who practices abomination and lying, shall ever come into it, but only those whose names are written in the lamb's book of life."

— Revelation 21:23-27

Practical Applications

- Choose your friends carefully. Have no soul ties with those that are ungodly, even if they are called 'Christians' but are not walking in holiness.
- Choose your spouse *very* carefully. A marriage covenant is binding for life. Make sure that you and your spouse are on the same 'page' spiritually. Many backsliding believers (mixed believers!) marry unbelievers and have miserable marriages. Make sure that you are not a backslider!

- Remove all traces of replacement theology from your life. Including the celebration of Christmas, Easter, Good Friday and Halloween. Burn all of its decorations.
- Get rid of any music, magazines, books, DVD's or videos that are ungodly and do not build you up in the spirit! Burn them.
- Get rid of all superstitious objects, even if it has sentimental value to you. Those bring curses and are normally connected with an ungodly soul tie. It is a type of witchcraft manipulation.
- Go around your home or your room and remove all decorations that are not holy and give no glory to Yah!
- Go around your home or your room and remove all decorations that are not holy and give no glory to Yah!
- Burn all jewels, clothing, pictures and love letters of unholy relationships! As long as you have them, these people can exercise spiritual influence and control over you!
- Get rid of all cigarettes and unholy incense! Smoking is not only deathly physically but it is a type of demonic worship. Repent of this (Even pipe smoking!) and ask Yah's help! He will help you *if* you are committed and do your best to obey Him! His Spirit will help you as you obey His Word!

- Get out of every ungodly financial alliance with unbelievers, even if they are family members. Seek His face and He will show you the peaceful way out. You may need to fast and pray to get a clear answer. Get un-busy and listen to Yah's voice.
- Get rid of all ungodly clothing. (Yes, burn them or destroy them.) Today most fashion is designed by homosexuals and they carry that spirit and style. Small shirts that expose bellies, bras, breasts and underwear are *not* godly! They are designed for sexual seduction. Miniskirts that expose your intimate parts are not Godly either! Be careful with your intimacy as a lady. If you are a man, be careful not to flaunt your manhood in a way that is sexually seductive! We can dress very beautifully without trying to be 'sexy' or worldly. We are called to be *holy*, separate, different and peculiar (1 Peter 2:9)
- Check what kind of job you are involved in. Do you have to compromise holiness in order to do it? One day, a believer I knew, told me that she was the secretary of a physician that performed abortions. Her job was to sign the order of abortion of babies! She was very tormented by doing that but still wanted the money her job provided! Please do not be an idolater. Let go of every ungodly job and trust Yah for a decent job that will bring Him glory! I'd rather clean the streets than be in a high position where I am required to break His Commandments!

King David said: *"For a day in thy courts is better than a thousand, I had rather be a doorkeeper in the house of my God, than to dwell in the tents of wickedness."* Psalm 84:10 KJV

- If you are put in a high position in government or finances, make sure that you do not break Yah's Commandments in order to please men and retain your position. Study the book of Daniel and the story of Joseph in the Book of Genesis and follow their godly example!

- When you buy clothes, see to it that there are no mixed organic fibers in them. (egg. Wool + Cotton, or Silk + Cotton) As long as there are labels, read labels and be picky with what you are buying. When Yah gave this statute about clothing, He knew what He was doing.

- If you have a garden, sow your seed orderly and not mixed and let the Most High bless your crop!

- If you are a minister: Be faithful to the message and the ministry that Yah has entrusted, you with and do not try to be like someone else because of your desire for acceptance. Be faithful in your field and He will reward you! Remember that holiness comes from your heart and mind! Watch what you put inside of you. Watch what you read, listen to and the TV programs that you see. Be discerning between the holy and the profane.

- Ask the precious Holy Spirit and be sensitive not to grieve Him. Pay attention to His signals inside of you. Reverend Katherine Kuhlman used to say, *"Do no grieve the Holy Spirit. He is all I have!"* She was one of the most anointed and powerful ministers of the gospel that ever lived. Remember, the Holy Spirit is *holy* and so are you!

A Disclaimer

God did not call you to judge and criticize people. Make sure that you change your own lifestyle and become an example to others. When needed instruct others in the ways of holiness in a spirit of meekness. And please remember that only the humble are open for good news. Do not cast your pearls before swine and do not be prideful. Your example should speak a loud message!

"For you are a chosen race, a royal priesthood, a holy nation, a people of God's own possession, so that you may proclaim the excellencies of Him who has called you out of darkness into His marvelous light."

— 1 Peter 2:9

CHAPTER FIFTEEN:

Sowing & Reaping

Creational Law Number Seven

The law of sowing and reaping was confirmed to Noah after the flood,

"While the earth remains, seedtime and harvest and cold and heat, and summer and winter, and day and night shall not cease."

— Genesis 8:22

I believe that this is by far the most important and revealing creational law as everything in life is directed by this law. Many people are very frustrated right now because they don't like their 'crops' in life. Instead of repenting, they become angry with God and humanity, feeling like victims of their circumstances and feeling sorry for themselves. And as they do that, they keep on going through the endless vicious circle of the curse!

Some people would ignore the law of sowing and reaping, the law of reciprocity. In the Apostolic writings it is described as follows,

"In everything, therefore, treat people the same way you want them to treat you, for this is the law and the prophets."

— Matthew 7:12

Sometimes people have come to me and told me, *"I don't feel any love in my congregation"* or *"I don't think anybody loves me"* or *"I am frustrated as no one wants to help me."* My answer to those complaints which are very common throughout the body of Messiah is this,

If you need someone to love you or to help you, you love them first and help them first! In other words, 'Sow plenty of love and helpfulness and very soon you will reap!'

However, when you sow, do not try to reap it from the same person! Your Father knows how to reward you, and He will bless you in due season.

Sow love, friendship, help, righteousness, finances, the Word without expecting them to return the kindness to you. Yah will see to it that you reap the right crop if you sow the right seed.

When I was in the USA one time, I heard the story of Johnny Apple Seed. This was a man that walked throughout many cities sowing apple seeds. He sowed and sowed...And one day many apple trees sprang up! I am sure he could not remember all the places he sowed into or even how many seeds he planted! However, the law of sowing and reaping was put into work and today there are many apple trees in the USA!

Begin to sow that which bears good fruit in and through your attitudes and behavior...

Sowing the Word

"For as the rain and the snow come down from heaven, and do not return there without watering the earth and making it bear and sprout, and furnishing seed to the sewer and bread to the eater; so will My Word be which goes forth from My mouth; It will not return to Me empty, without accomplishing what I desire, and without succeeding in the matter for which I sent it."

— Isaiah 55:10, 11

You cannot expect to be a faith filled person, with godly attitudes and reactions if you do not spend time sowing the Word of Yah into your heart and mind! Do not expect quick results! Sometimes they happen, but most of the time diligence and perseverance are required, in order to let His Word in through all the lies that we have believed, and the ungodly patterns that we have internalized. Miracles happen every day; however, there are many miracle processes in the making! Do not get discouraged if you do not see instant crops. Remember that after the seed goes into the ground, it grows underground, and you can't see it until it springs up.

This could take some time! Be like Johnny Apple Seed and keep sowing and keep watering with Word prayers.

"And let us not be weary in well doing; for in due season we shall reap if we faint not."

— Galatians 6:9

Make sure to remove the weeds that grow in your field. Be merciless with these following "weeds",

- Discouragement
- Unbelief
- Disappointment
- Unforgiveness
- Bitterness
- Self-righteousness
- Pride
- Cynicism
- Skepticism
- Frustration
- Weariness
- Depression

If you are experiencing any of these, enter into a time of prayer (and fasting as needed) and seek your Father in heaven to set you free from the lies that you have believed. Then return to shalom, faith and hope and keep sowing!

Practical Applications

- Sow the Word into your spirit day and night. Meditate constantly on His Word. Speak it out loud to yourself, pray it, sing it and *do it*. This is the road to wholeness and prosperity. Joshua 1:8

- Sow attitudes of love and mercy to others. Be very forgiving.
- Sow financially in the correct manner. What belongs to the poor give to the poor, and what belongs to God's ministers, given to them!
- Remember to keep on sowing *good*, even if people do you *evil*. (Read all of Matthew 5, 6 and 7)
- Watch what your lips say, the power of death and life is in the tongue! (Proverbs 18:21, James 3). If you prophesy evil, disease, poverty to yourself or to others, that is what you are going to reap! Be careful to be honest but yet speak what is righteous in Yah's eyes, according to His Word and promises.
- Sow good, respectful, honorable manners even unto the simplest people.
- Treat those under you with love and respect. Expect the best out of them. Sow good expectations.
- Sow yourself in the altar of Yah and see God reproduce many disciples like you. (Read Romans 12:1-2)
- Overcome all evil crops of your past with *good* and *God* crops in your present and future. Regardless of how much time it takes, it will never fail. Light is stronger than darkness.

A great pastor told me one day that he used to have a terrible marriage. He used to criticize his wife all the time. It was so bad that she used to serve him cold breakfast! He spent many nights sleeping on the living room sofa. One day the Holy

Spirit told him, *"Stop criticizing your wife."* He began to obey the holy one and stopped sowing critical words. However, his wife did not change right away; only after two years did she stop being angry with her husband and accepted him. Today they have a great marriage! It took two years to overcome the evil crop with the good one. Sometimes it takes longer, so do not quit sowing *good*!

A special word:

The Sowing of Ruth

"May Yahveh reward your work, and your wages from Yahveh, the God of Israel, under whose wings you have come to seek refuge?"

— Ruth 2:12

These powerful words were spoken by Boaz to Ruth and they came to pass! They were spoken because Ruth had been sowing unconditional love to her suffering Jewish mother in law, Naomi. Eventually, Ruth married wealthy and influential Boaz and became the most influential woman in Bethlehem though a cursed Moabite.

Her sowing of love unto a Jew caused her whole life and future generations to change! She is mentioned in Matthew one as one of the two women in the royal lineage of Messiah. The other woman is Rahab who helped the Hebrew spies in Jericho.

The sowing of most of the church in the last 1600 years concerning the Jews has been terrible. Yah is calling the

Ecclesia to be as Ruth to Israel and to the Jewish people and to overcome the evil sowing and crop of curses, with the *Ruth kind of sowing*. He is calling the Gentile grafted in Christians to sow their lives into the healing and prosperity of Israel. Thus, they will enter in the blessing of Abraham.

Many curses have fallen on the church and on the nations for hating the Jews, for opposing their return to the land and for rejecting Torah and the Jewish roots of the faith. As you become *grafted in*, you can overcome this evil crop with a *good, glorious crop* of *many sheep nations*! This means to do good, speak well and think well of Israel.

"I will bless those who bless you, and the one who curses you I will curse. And in you all the families of the earth will be blessed."

— Genesis 12:3

A Final Prayer

Dear Father in heaven, thank You for speaking *truth* into my spirit. I am willing to change and improve my sowing! From now on I will be like a Ruth to Israel and will do her good with all my heart. I sow myself as a Ruth (man or woman!) to bring healing and restoration to Your Jewish people worldwide and to help bring this End time message of "grafted in", into all the church and nations of the world. Here I am YHVH. *Hineni!* In Yeshua's name. Amen.

CLOSING WORD:

Jerusalem Our Mother

"Be joyful with Jerusalem and rejoice for her all you who love her; be exceedingly glad with her all you who mourn for her. That you may nurse and be satisfied with her comforting breasts, that you may suck and be delighted with her bountiful bosom. For thus says Yahveh, 'Behold I extend peace to her like a river, and the glory of the nations like an overflowing stream. And you will be nursed; you will be carried on the hip and fondled on the knees. As one whom his mother comforts, so I will comfort you; and you will be comforted in Jerusalem."

— Isaiah 66:10-13

The only way that we can be comforted is when we are mothered and fathered properly. For too long, the father of lies, the devil, and Mother Babylon have parented the church through replacement theology. It is time to be restored to our true mother, Jerusalem-Israel and to our true Father Yahveh, the God of Israel and the Jewish Messiah!

Let me ask you a challenging question; how much lying is acceptable? How many lies can we contain as disciples of

Messiah and as Sons of the Most High? Is it worth our while to pay the price to get rid of all lies, we believe? Is *truth* an absolute or does it depend on the culture one comes from? Can real truth cross all cultural and religious barriers and bring real freedom? The Word tells us that only when we know the truth intimately, are we made free (John 8:32). It also says that we should buy the truth and not sell it or relinquish it in order to appease ourselves or others.

Truth is costly, but without truth we will stay sick, insignificant and confused. To keep on believing lies is very dangerous! It can cause your death and the death of others. The belief in replacement theology in any of its versions has killed and destroyed too many people! *"Buy the truth and sell it not!"* (Proverbs 23:23)

Today there are multitudes of people that suffer from depression due to a confused identity. They have believed so many lies about who they are that these lies keep them tormented. Then they run to psychologists and to psychiatric drugs to get help and they can never get healed. These treatments at best keep them quiet and drugged but not whole. The healing of one's identity is extremely important!

For many years my own daughter suffered from a confused identity as she was told by others that she was not to relate to me as her mother anymore and that she should have nothing to do with me or my Yeshua! Day and night, she was fed those lies as she was growing up, until finally at the age of twelve, and after many family tragedies, she began to develop a clinical depression and she was treated by professionals.

However even doctors cannot cure this condition! Finally, as Israel was celebrating her Jubilee, her 50th year, Adí, (whose name means my jewel), was at the climax of her depression. She was now turning 15, and for ten years she was told by well-meaning relatives that she should deny me and my God! Her identity was deeply confused. She did not know who she was anymore. She hated me and hated my Messiah who she had known previously when she was five and she was with me.

Adí was afraid of everything, of life, of me and of the future. She was tormented day and night and due to that, she spent time in and out of treatment for almost five years of her life. She was given almost every treatment imaginable, but nothing helped! Her father had taken his life due to mental disease and it looked as if she was going to follow him...But Yah! Glory be to His holy name!

After many years of prayer for my daughter, the Father in heaven healed her confused identity and she recognized me as her mother and began to open her heart to the Messiah.

I remember after 4 years of this ordeal, during which I had been told that her mind would never be restored and that she might never be herself again, that doctor looked at me with very sad eyes and said: *"I can give you no hope for your daughter, she is responding to no treatment."* To which I answered encouraging the doctor who looked hopeless and depressed: *"Dear doctor, you keep on doing what you know to do, and I will keep on doing what I know to do and my God will rescue her."*

Sure enough, around one and a half years later, my daughter's depression left, and she was granted a certificate that described her condition as being in *full remission*! Adí had received her miracle! Though she still needed to do checkups in order to 'prevent' a reoccurrence, Adí was sane! Then she began to be restored to life after five years of this terrifying journey. She enrolled into college and began to study, and she became one of the best students! This was the girl that doctors diagnosed as having lost her intellectual abilities. One day as she was in a psychology class, the teacher asked all the class: *"Who is your role model in life? Who is your example?"* Most of the students had pop or rock stars as their role model, such as Michael Jackson and Madonna. None of the students mentioned a parent as a role model. However, my daughter rose up in class and said these awesome words: *"My mother is my role model; she is my example in life."* Her identity had come to rest and so did her soul.

In the same manner for over 1.700 years the church has been lied to about her identity. Since the Council of Nicea and the Gentile church Fathers, she has been told to reject the Jews and everything Jewish. She has hated her own mother, Jerusalem by killing her offspring the Jewish people through pogroms, crusades, inquisitions and the Holocaust. She has hated the godly instructions of her mother as written in the Hebrew Holy Scriptures, calling them 'Old Testament' and decreeing that they are done away with!

The church has confusion in her identity for instead of identifying with Jerusalem, replacement theology has caused her to have a Babylonian identity. Thus, the church is sick, tormented, divided and confused!

Since Israel's Jubilee, the shofar call went out to restore the church back to her original mother, to Jerusalem and to the Apostolic Jewish foundations of the faith, to the love of Israel! At the same time that my own daughter was receiving treatment for a misplaced identity, so was the church called to the treatment room of Yah, to be restored to her mother and her mother's God, the God of Israel. The Jewish Messiah versus the universal Christ and Gentile Messiah. The shofar call has already gone out to the Ecclesia in the nations, to repent from replacement theology and the Babylonian gospel, and to go back to the original gospel of the Kingdom as preached by the Jewish Apostles 2000 years ago! The grace of Yah is poured out now through signs, wonders and miracles in order to restore His bride to wholeness. The Ecclesia is being released from the torment of a deceptive Babylonian identity into the *freedom* of her identity with Israel, with the Jewish people as grafted into the olive tree! Her testimony of wholeness, the glory that will be within her, the greatness of Yah restored in her will cause Israel to see Messiah and for many nations to turn to Yah and to become *sheep nations*!

"Then I saw a new heaven and a new earth; for the first heaven and the first earth passed away, and there is no longer any sea. And I saw the Holy city the New Jerusalem. Coming down out of heaven from God, made ready as a bride adorned for her husband... Having the glory of God, her brilliance was like a costly stone, as a stone of crystal clear

jasper... It had a great and high wall, with twelve gates, and at the gates twelve angels and names were written on them, which are the names of the twelve tribes of the Sons of Israel. And the wall of the city had twelve foundation stones, and on them were the twelve names of the twelve apostles of the Lamb...The nations will walk by its light, and the kings of the earth will bring their glory into it; and nothing unclean, and no one who practices abomination and lying shall ever come into it, but only those whose names are written in the Lamb's book of life."

— Revelation 21:1-27

I pray that this book will be a tool in the hands of the Almighty to restore His daughter, His jewel (His Adí), His Ecclesia to wholeness, to *shalom*. That she in turn will bring Israel and the Jewish people, who are suffering from a confused identity due to much suffering and sin to reconciliation with Messiah, to deliverance and restoration, to become the chief sheep nation of many other *sheep nations!*

"For I do not want you brethren, to be uninformed of this mystery – so that you will not be wise in your own estimation-that a partial hardening has happened to Israel until the fullness of the Gentiles has come in; and so all Israel will be saved; just as it is written: "The deliverer will come from Zion, He will remove ungodliness from Jacob. This is My Covenant with them when I take away their sins."

— Romans 11:25-27

In His all-encompassing love;
Archbishop Dr. Dominiquae Bierman Israel

A Prayer of Greatness & Success

I thank You, Father in heaven, that I am Your new creation child through Yeshua the Jewish Messiah. Thank You that I am fruitful and am multiplying, that I replenish the earth and fill it with more people like me who live & worship You in Spirit and truth. Thank You that I subdue and conquer the earth and all earthly problems and circumstances and that I have dominion over all things created. (Genesis 1:28)

Thank You, Father, that I am more honorable than others because I do not yield to my adverse circumstances but believe in Your goodness—that you bless me indeed, that you enlarge my territory and my sphere of influence and make me very prosperous. Thank You that Your hand and all Your support and ability are with me. Thank You that you keep me from evil that I may not have any more grief and sadness in my life. (1 Chronicles 4:9, 10). Thank You that you are making a great nation of me, that You are blessing me and making my name great. Thank You for making me a blessing, that You bless those who bless me and that You curse those who take me lightly and dishonor me. Thank You that in me and through me all the families, ethnic groups and nations of the earth are being blessed. (Genesis 12:2, 3). Thank You that because I keep Your Commandments and teach others to do so I am called *great* in the Kingdom of heaven and I am blessed, prosperous and successful everywhere I go and in whatever I do. Both myself and my children and all those that are under my care are always blessed and always on top of things. We are greatly successful! (Matthew 5:17-20, Deuteronomy 28:1-14)

APPENDIX I

Two Weddings & One Divorce

The First Marriage

The following illustration will explain why Christianity was 'the womb' of the Spanish Inquisition, the Crusades, and the Nazi Holocaust. Yahveh-God is looking to the church for repentance in order to influence the nations and fulfill the mandate of Matthew 28:19 *"Go and make disciples of all nations."*

The first and original church was married to a Jewish Husband by the name of Yeshua the Messiah & into His family the Jewish people (Ephesians 2:14 and Romans 11). The Wedding Ceremony took place in Jerusalem. It was ratified and sealed by the spilling of the blood of the Husband and by the breaking of His body. (Luke 22:15–20) The time of this marriage was the holy biblical Feast of Passover. The fruit of this miraculous wedding was thousands and thousands of people, both Jews and Gentiles, saved and healed. Even the shadow of this holy bride healed the sick, as signs and wonders and miracles followed her wherever she went in the name of her Husband Yeshua.

This marriage led the wife to much suffering. Many in the world did not love her Husband and tried to kill her by persecuting her and even throwing her to the lions during the Roman Empire's reign of terror. Those were hard years. After many years of suffering, Yeshua's wife had become weary. He had gone to prepare a place for her and had not come back yet.

She started to get tired from her lifestyle as an outcast, persecuted and hunted at every corner. She longed for peace at any price. She longed for the warm embrace of a Husband who would provide her with peace and security here on this earth... At her weakest point an earthly king appeared. (Matthew 10:34, John 14:27, Jeremiah 8:11)

This earthly king was influential and powerful by earthly standards. He could stop the killing and persecution against her. He could give her the security she longed for... *If* only she would agree to divorce this Jewish Husband of hers and completely separate from His family Israel, and from that Book that she treasured so much – where He had left her all of His instructions and the family legacy of God's Word.

This powerful king seemed to be a spiritual man. He claimed that her Jewish Husband had appeared to him in a dream and had given him the crown of the Roman Empire. His deceptive charm and appeasing manners managed to attract the very weary bride of Messiah, but not all were deceived. There was a portion of the bride/church/ecclesia that was not fooled by the charms of this deceitful king. These were the Messianic Jews of the time.

They were too rooted in the writings of the Holy Book and the ancient Hebrew Scriptures to be deceived. But the vast majority of the believers at that time were Gentiles, and they did not want any more suffering on behalf of the Book, its Author, or His family.

They wanted freedom and peace at all cost.

The powerful Constantine sang the song of peace and safety and prepared a bed of roses... The Gentile portion of the church slept with him, falling into violent adultery and wounding the heart of her heavenly Jewish Husband. In order to appease the conscience of this adulterous church, Constantine decided to legalize this unholy union in the year AD 325 by means of a wedding ceremony called the Council of Nicaea and drawing up an ungodly and illegal marriage contract called the Nicean Creed.

He used his worldly power to draw all the gentile church fathers, which for the most part were already anti-Semitic and hated their Jewish roots. These church fathers were to be witnesses of this horrendous divorce and the adulterous new marriage between the predominantly Gentile church and another Jesus, a product of Constantine's own creation.

This alternative Savior came with another family, another book (totally disconnected from the ancient Hebrew writings), other customs, Laws, festivals, traditions and ways of measuring time.

Knowing that his brand-new wife was accustomed to worshipping God, he organized for her a god that would suit her perfectly by not demanding any holiness from her. He presented a god of peace that was lenient towards a mixture of paganism and holiness: An all-inclusive god, who accepted all traditions and blended them into one.

Now Passover and First Fruits, the festival of Yeshua's resurrection, would become The Feast of Ishtar, the goddess of fertility, or Easter with bunny rabbits and Easter eggs. (At that time eggs were dipped in the blood of the babies sacrificed to the goddess, thus the tradition of painting the eggs).

Now the fay of worship would change from Shabbat to Sunday in order to eternalize the sun god who for now would be called Jesus – yet it was another Jesus and certainly not Yeshua, the Jewish Messiah.

Then the day of the winter solstice of witchcraft, called Saturnalia or Paganalia, celebrated on the 25th of December in the Roman Empire, was to acquire the name Christmas and would celebrate the birth of this false Messiah. For the true Messiah was born during the holy biblical Feast of Tabernacles and followed the Hebrew biblical calendar, not the Roman one. (Daniel 7:25–27, Jeremiah 10:2–4 about the Christmas tree.)

The ancient Holy Book of the Hebrew Scriptures was to become obsolete, and its Laws done away with. Instead, Constantine compiled the apostolic writings, the letters of Paul and others into a new holy book and called it the New Testament. He gave this holy book his own perverse interpretation, completely divorced from the foundational

Hebrew Writings whom he and his followers called the 'Old Testament.' (Matthew 5:17–21)

"In rejecting their custom, we may transmit to our descendants the legitimate way of celebrating Easter... We ought not therefore to have anything in common with the Jew, for the Savior has shown us another way; our worship following a more legitimate and more convenient course (the order of the days of the week); And consequently, in unanimously adopting this mode, we desire dearest brethren to separate ourselves from the detestable company of the Jew." (Excerpt from *The Nicene Creed*, year 325, found in *Eusebius, Vita Const. Lib III 18-20)*

This creed and its instructions are still followed by most Christians today with the celebration of Easter, Christmas, Sunday (replacing Shabbat), and the rejection of the Laws of God.

Indeed, a new religion had been born. It had a gentile god by the name of Jesus Christ, an apostle by the name of Constantine, a new book by the name of the New Testament (although compiled from the apostolic writings, which are completely Yah-inspired, it was deceitfully interpreted through gentile eyes and gentile theologians), and new traditions, and unholy festivals such as Easter, Christmas, Sunday, and Halloween.

And most importantly... *no Jews*... no, not even the Messiah.

What has been the fruit of this adulterous marriage?

Either make the tree good and its fruit good, or else make the tree bad and its fruit bad; for a tree is known by its fruit.

— Matthew 12:33

The fruit of the first holy matrimony were salvations and healings. The fruit of this ungodly and pagan marriage were forced conversions and killings, yes even mass destructions of the family of Yeshua the Messiah, (the true Husband), in the name of the false Jesus Christ god created by Constantine.

A god who, according to Constantine in the Nicene Creed, had shown us *another way*. What was that way? It is a way of jealousy, hatred, killing, destruction, and Lawlessness. Horrendous Christian events such as pogroms, the holy inquisition, and the holocaust, have taken place since this ungodly 4th century marriage and the creation of this false religion.

The hatred conveyed in the Nicene Creed against the Jews and anything Jewish, including the Torah and the Old Testament, has continued through the great Protestant Reformation of the 16th century, and it still influences Christians today.

The following excerpt is from *Our Hands are Stained with Blood* by Michael Brown, as he quotes directly from Martin Luther's writings.

Luther wrote this after he was frustrated from trying to evangelize the Jews and when he was old and sick:

"What shall we Christians do with this damned rejected

race of Jews? First, their synagogues should be set on fire. Secondly, their homes should likewise be broken down and destroyed. Thirdly, they should be deprived of their prayer books and Talmud's. Fourthly, their rabbis must be forbidden under threat of death to teach anymore. Fifthly, passports and traveling privileges should be absolutely forbidden to the Jews... To sum up dear princes and nobles, who have Jews in your domains, if this advice of mine does not suit you, then find a better one. So that you and we may all be free of this insufferable, devilish burden – the Jews." (Luther and Brown)

Hitler followed Luther's instructions meticulously and quoted him while doing so. The fruit? Over six million Jews exterminated in horrendous death camps and gas chambers, and many survivors scarred for life.

Prophetic Altar Call

After two days He will revive us; on the third day He will raise us up, that we may live in His sight. Let us know; let us pursue the knowledge of Yahveh. His going forth is established as the morning; He will come to us like the rain, like the latter and former rain to the earth.

— Hosea 6:2-3

The Third Day is upon us, the Third Millennium, and this is the Father's call to His Third Day church:

Come let us return to Yeshua, to our Jewish Messiah, His Jewish family and His ancient Hebrew Scriptures. Come let us reinterpret the New Testament through the eyes of the holy Scriptures. Let us separate ourselves from our pagan husband, Constantine, and his false Jesus and let us go back to the true Messiah Yeshua, to His Father's Laws and Precepts, to true divine holy grace, to true love and holiness. Let us return to Jerusalem, and let us be made whole from centuries of adultery and paganism, as we go back to the original apostolic Jewish roots of our faith.

In Yeshua's love and brokenness;

Archbishop Dr. Dominiquae & Rabbi Baruch Bierman

Disclaimer: What this Article is Not Saying

- It is *not* saying to go back to the laws of Rabbinic Judaism.
- It is *not* implying that all Christians have anti-Semitism.
- It is *not* disqualifying the countless believers who call on the name of Jesus Christ meaning the *true* Jewish Messiah Yeshua.
- It is *not* disqualifying worship on Sunday, Monday, Tuesday or any other day.
- It is *not* disqualifying the New Testament as Bible (Only the wrong, 'divorced' interpretations of it).

BIBLIOGRAPHY

"C. Difficile Superbugs in Meat | NutritionFacts.Org." @ *nutrition_facts*, 15 Apr. 2015, nutritionfacts.org/video/c-difficile-superbugs-in-meat/. Accessed 7 July 2020.

"Chronic Headaches & Pork Tapeworms | NutritionFacts. Org." *Nutritionfacts.Org,* nutritionfacts.org/video/chronic-headaches-and-pork-tapeworms/. Accessed 7 July 2020.

"The Holocaust and the Christian World." store.yadvashem. org/the-holocaust-and-the-christian-world-16. Accessed 7 July 2020.

Bierman, Dominiquae. *The Healing Power of the Roots.* Jerusalem, Kad-Esh Map Ministries International, 1997.

Brown, Michael L. *Our Hands Are Stained with Blood : The Tragic Story of the Church and the Jewish People.* Shippensburg, Pa, Destiny Image Publishers, Inc, 2019.

Carroll, Robert P, and Stephen Prickett. T*he Bible : Authorized King James Version.* Oxford ; New York, Oxford University Press, 2008.

Excerpt from *The Nicene Creed,* year 325, found in *Eusebius, Vita Const. Lib III 18-20)*

Forlenza, O. V., et al. "Psychiatric Manifestations of Neurocysticercosis: A Study of 38 Patients from a

Neurology Clinic in Brazil." *Journal of Neurology, Neurosurgery, and Psychiatry,* vol. 62, no. 6, 1 June 1997, pp. 612–616, www.ncbi.nlm.nih.gov/pubmed/9219748, 10.1136/jnnp.62.6.612. Accessed 7 July 2020.

"In the Midst of All Shaking... – Christian Friends of Israel-USA." *Cfi-Usa.Org,* 2020, cfi-usa.org/in-the-midst-of-all-shaking/. Accessed 6 July 2020.

Jewish Publication Society. *JPS Hebrew-English Tanakh : The Traditional Hebrew Text and the New JPS Translation.* Philadelphia, Jewish Publication Society, 1999.

Lockman Foundation. *Bible. New American Standard Bible.* Editorial: Nashville, Holman Bible Publ, 1986.

Luther, Martin, and Texe W Marrs. *On the Jews and Their Lies.* Austin, Tx, Rivercrest Pub, 2014.

Rittner, Carol, Stephen D. Smith, Irena Steinfeldt, and Yehûdā Bauer. *The Holocaust and the Christian World: Reflections on the Past, Challenges for the Future.* New York: Paulist Press, 2019.

Sotelo, Julio. "Clinical Manifestations, Diagnosis, and Treatment of Neurocysticercosis." *Current Neurology and Neuroscience Reports,* vol. 11, no. 6, 15 Sept. 2011, pp. 529–535, 10.1007/s11910-011-0226-7. Accessed 22 Oct. 2019.

Terrye Goldblum Seedman. *Holy to Yahveh.* Debary, FL, Longwood Communications, 1996.

APPENDIX II
Other Books

Order now online: www.ZionsGospel.com

The MAP Revolution (Free E-Book)
Exposing Theologies that Obstruct the Bride

The Identity Theft
The Return of the 1st Century Messiah

The Healing Power of the Roots
It's a Matter of Life or Death!

Sheep Nations
It's Time to Take the Nations!

Restoring the Glory: The Original Way
The Ancient Paths Rediscovered

Stormy Weather
Judgment Has Already Begun,
Revival is Knocking at the Door

Yeshua is the Name
The Important Restoration of the Original
Hebrew Name of the Messiah

The Bible Cure for Africa and the Nations
The Key to the Restoration of All Africa

The Key of Abraham
The Blessing or the Curse?

Yes!
The Dramatic Salvation Story of Archbishop
Dr. Dominiquae Bierman

Eradicating the Cancer of Religion
Hint: All People Have It

Restoration of Holy Giving
Releasing the True 1,000 Fold Blessing

Vision Negev
The Awesome Restoration of the Sephardic Jews

Defeating Depression
This Book is a Kiss from Heaven

From Sickology to a Healthy Logic
The Product of 18 Years Walking Through
Psychiatric Hospitals

ATG: Addicts Turning to God
The Biblical Way to Handle Addicts and Addictions

The Woman Factor by Rabbi Baruch Bierman

Freedom From Womanphobia

The Revival of the Third Day (Free E-Book)

The Return to Yeshua the Jewish Messiah

Tribute to the Jew in You Music Book

Notes for the Tribute to the Jew in You Music Album

Music Albums

www.zionsgospel.com

The Key of Abraham

Abba Shebashamayim

Uru

Retorno

Tribute to the Jew in You

Tribute to the Jew in You Instrumental

Get Equipped & Partner with Us

Global Revival MAP (GRM) Israeli Bible School

Take the most life-changing video Bible school online that focuses on restoring the gospel of the 1st century.

For more information or to order, please contact us:

www.grmbibleschool.com

grm@dominiquaebierman.com

United Nations for Israel Movement

We invite you to join us as a member and partner with $25 a month, which supports the advancing of this End time vision that will bring true unity to the body of the Messiah. We will see the One New Man form, witness the restoration of Israel, and take part in the birthing of SHEEP NATIONS. Today is an exciting time to be serving Him!

www.unitednationsforisrael.org

info@unitednationsforisrael.org

Global Re-Education Initiative (GRI) Against Anti-Semitism

Discover the Jewishness of the Messiah and defeat Christian anti-Semitism with this online video course to see revival in your nation!

www.against-antisemitism.com

info@against-antisemitism.com

Join Our Annual Israel Tours

Travel through the Holy Land and watch the Hebrew Holy Scriptures come alive.

www.kad-esh.org/tours-and-events/

To Send Offerings to Support our Work

Your help keeps this mission of restoration going far and wide.

www.kad-esh.org/donations

CONTACT US

Archbishop Dr. Dominiquae & Rabbi Baruch Bierman

Kad-Esh MAP Ministries | www.kad-esh.org
info@kad-esh.org

United Nations for Israel | www.unitednationsforisrael.org
info@unitednationsforisrael.org

RESOURCES

Zion's Gospel Press | www.zionsgospel.com
shalom@zionsgospel.com | +1-972-301-7087
52 Tuscan Way, Ste 202-412, St. Augustine
Florida, 32092, USA

Made in the USA
Middletown, DE
21 October 2022